A. S. Byatt's
Possession

CONTINUUM CONTEMPORARIES

Also available in this series:

Pat Barker's *Regeneration*, by Karin Westman
Kazuo Ishiguro's *The Remains of the Day*, by Adam Parkes
Carol Shields's *The Stone Diaries*, by Abby Werlock
J. K. Rowling's *Harry Potter Novels*, by Philip Nel
Jane Smiley's *A Thousand Acres*, by Susan Farrell
Barbara Kingsolver's *The Poisonwood Bible*, by Linda Wagner-Martin
Louis De Bernieres's *Captain Corelli's Mandolin*, by Con Coroneos
Irvine Welsh's *Trainspotting*, by Robert Morace
Donna Tartt's *The Secret History*, by Tracy Hargreaves
Toni Morrison's *Paradise*, by Kelly Reames
Don DeLillo's *Underworld*, by John Duvall
Annie Proulx's *The Shipping News*, by Aliki Varvogli
Graham Swift's *Last Orders*, by Pamela Cooper
Haruki Murakami's *The Wind-up Bird Chronicle*, by Matthew Strecher
Ian Rankin's *Black and Blue*, by Gill Plain
Bret Easton Ellis's *American Psycho*, by Julian Murphet
Cormac McCarthy's *All the Pretty Horses*, by Stephen Tatum
Iain Banks's *Complicity*, by Cairns Craig
Michael Ondaatje's *The English Patient*, by John Bolland

Forthcoming in this series:

David Guterson's *Snow Falling on Cedars*, by Jennifer Haytock
Helen Fielding's *Bridget Jones' Diary*, by Imelda Whelehan
Sebatian Faulks's *Birdsong*, by Pat Wheeler
Kate Atkinson's *Behind the Scenes at the Museum*, by Emma Parker
Hanif Kureishi's *The Buddha of Suburbia*, by Nahem Yousaf
Jonathan Coe's *What a Carve Up!*, by Pamela Thurschwell
Nick Hornby's *High Fidelity*, by Joanne Knowles
Zadie Smith's *White Teeth*, by Claire Squires
Arundhati Roy's *The God of Small Things*, by Julie Mullaney
Alan Warner's *Morvern Callar*, by Sophy Dale
Margaret Atwood's *Alias Grace*, by Gina Wisker
Vikram Seth's *A Suitable Boy*, by Angela Atkins

· **A. S. BYATT'S**

Possession

A READER'S GUIDE

CATHERINE BURGASS

CONTINUUM | NEW YORK | LONDON

2002

The Continuum International Publishing Group Inc
370 Lexington Avenue, New York, NY 10017

The Continuum International Publishing Group Ltd
The Tower Building, 11 York Road, London SE1 7NX

www.continuumbooks.com

Printed in the United States of America

Library of Congress Cataloging-in-Publication Data

Burgass, Catherine.
    A.S. Byatt's Possession : a reader's guide / Catherine Burgass.
      p. cm. — (Continuum contemporaries)
    Includes bibliographical references.
    ISBN 0-8264-5248-5 (pbk. : alk. paper)
    1. Byatt, A. S. (Antonia Susan), 1936– Possession. I. Title. II. Series.

PR6052.Y2 P63 2002
823'.914—dc21

                                                          2001048684

Contents

· 1

The Novelist

A. S. Byatt rejects the academic tendency to reduce literary works to a convenient label. In both her personal and professional life, she has worked assiduously towards encompassing what are frequently regarded as mutually exclusive states: a successful career and family life; criticism and creative writing; a fiction both intellectual and sensual, realist and romantic. *Possession* represents the realisation of this ambition, since it managed to please nearly everybody—academics, critics, and ordinary readers—by means of its diversity and won its author a significant degree of fame and fortune. It is a novel which, in common with many successful postmodern fictions, is complex enough to lend itself to sophisticated critical analysis, yet manages to cater to the recreational reader. It includes, in its 550-odd pages, an astonishing variety of literary forms woven into an intricately constructed plot, and addresses esoteric intellectual questions while retaining traditional elements of story, well-realized scenes and well-rounded characters. Byatt's fiction has, from the first, been preoccupied with the tensions between different ways of writing and living; this section will focus on the evolution of these thematic and formal issues—from unresolved conflict in her first novel towards reconciliation in *Possession*.

THE LIFE AND THE WORK

A. S. Byatt was born Antonia Susan Drabble on 24 August 1936, in Sheffield, to John Drabble and Kathleen (Marie) Drabble, *née* Bloor. Both her parents had "bettered themselves" through education, and had graduated from Cambridge University. But for Byatt's mother this education had resulted in frustrated ambition when marriage and children precluded any kind of career. Byatt has described the atmosphere at home as unhappy; her mother was unable to control her bitterness, and conveyed to her children not only her own dissatisfaction, but her high expectations. Byatt grew up in this fraught domestic atmosphere an introverted and asthmatic child and a bookish high-achiever. Just as Roland experiences a disconcerting sense of his actions being determined by a romance plot in *Possession*, Byatt conceives of her life in terms of literary narrative. As a child, she identified with characters in fairy tales and myths of a literate household. This identification may not be unusual, but Byatt placed herself in the imaginative world of stories more firmly than many. Her mother's vicarious ambition was fulfilled; both Byatt and her sister, the novelist Margaret Drabble, have highly successful literary careers, though the press reports a kind of literary sibling rivalry, to Byatt's irritation.

While biographical readings of literary texts are regarded as slightly suspect in the academy, in Byatt's case a special plea can be made. Byatt herself believes that it is easier to penetrate the mind of a writer through his or her work than through superficial conversation. She has said of Iris Murdoch, with whom she was accustomed to lunch: "She knew I knew her secret self, which she had made public in her novels. And I knew I knew it, but the conversations remained the polite conversations of two women who liked each other but were not that intimate." In *Possession*, the two literary sleuths express a certain high-minded distaste for prying into the private lives of their subjects, which is born of a sense of decorum and their critical detachment. But in Byatt's fiction perennial thematic concerns clearly reflect her particular socio-historical location, and there is a significant part of the work which is semi autobiographical.

CREATIVITY/DOMESTICITY

As an educated middle-class woman coming of age in the post-war period Byatt faced certain conflicts in her own life which she repeatedly addresses in the novels. Byatt was subject to her mother's high expectations and was told at the age of five that she *would* go to Cambridge University, but further education was raising the expectations of a growing number of women. The expectations of society, however, were still such that these women were likely to marry young and follow the domestic pattern of their mothers' generation—a particularly unfortunate model for Byatt. She says in her preface to *The Shadow of the Sun* that all her novels "think about the problem of female vision, female art and thought," but this female vision is often occluded by domesticity, specifically the demands of dependent beings.

Byatt was apparently aware early of the inevitable loss of autonomy and the life of the mind occasioned by marriage. In her collection of essays *On Histories and Stories*, she describes the way that this loss is allegorized in fairy tales, where the princess is always kissed by the prince, released from her solitary confinement, and re-enters the human cycle of birth and death. Her response as a child was unconventional:

I think I knew even then, that there was something secretly good, illicitly desirable, about the ice-hills and glass barriers. [. . .] There was something wonderful about being beautiful and shining and high up with a lap full of golden fruit, something which was lost with human love, with the descent to be kissed and given away.

Nevertheless, Byatt was of the generation for whom to remain un-married would have been something rather pitiful. She writes, again in the preface to *The Shadow of the Sun*: "We wanted marriage and children, we wanted weddings and romantic love and sex, and to be normal." Continuing her self-location in terms of fairy story, she states:

The frozen, stony women became my images of choosing the perfection of the work, rejecting (so it seemed to me then, though I have done my best to keep my apple and swallow it). The imposed biological cycle, blood, kiss, roses, birth, death, and the hungry generation.

Byatt was a part of a particularly hungry generation of post-war women who sometimes managed to combine both family and ca-reer, though not without difficulties.

While educational institutions gave with one hand, raising con-sciousness and expectations, they reflected social norms by taking away with the other. Byatt gave up her doctoral research when she married her first husband, Ian Byatt in 1959. This decision may have been informed by the fact that the University customarily divested married women of their grants. It appears at this point that Byatt might have followed in her mother's footsteps — she produced two children in quick succession. But procreation did not, in her case, stifle the life of the mind and she completed *The Shadow of the Sun*, which she had begun as an undergraduate at Cambridge:

The novel was finished when I was a very desperate faculty wife in Durham. I had two children in two years—I was 25, and I thought I was old, "past it." [. . .] I began contriving—I sat rocking my son with one hand in a plastic chair on the table, and wrote with the other. I had a cleaning-lady, and ran across the Palace Green to the University for the hour she was there to write, fiercely, with a new desperation.

This contriving had results, and *Shadow of a Sun* was published in 1964. She writes in the 1991 preface: "I didn't want to write a 'me novel,'" but the novel dramatizes the oedipal and existential struggle of the isolated adolescent heroine Anna to establish herself and realize her artistic potential in the shadow of her genius writer father Henry Severell. This potential is signaled by means of a pervasive light symbolism, and is established through Anna's ability to perceive significance in mundane objects. Her vision occurs at night in a thunderstorm—literal and metaphorical illumination—but never sees the light of day. Anna has been tutored by her father's critical acolyte, Oliver, and gets into Cambridge University. This brings about a specifically female dilemma in that while she is studying there, they start a sexual relationship and Anna becomes pregnant. After much vacillation, which conveys at least the illusion of autonomy, she passively accepts Oliver as her fate.

Byatt's next novel, *The Game* (1967), which she had begun while at Bryn Mawr and continued while writing *Shadow of a Sun*, also alludes to the difficulties of achieving both domestic harmony and professional success. The antagonists here are two sisters: Julia, a successful women's novelist who is married with a daughter; and Cassandra, a mediaeval scholar at Oxford, whose domestic life is characterized by a nun-like austerity. At the close of the novel Julia's marriage has broken down and Cassandra has killed herself, signaling degrees of failure for both women. At this point Byatt's own professional life was apparently flourishing; she had been teaching in the Extra-Mural Department of London University since 1962, and at the Central School of Art since 1965. As well as the two novels, she had published a critical study of Iris Murdoch's fiction, *Degrees of Freedom* (1965). Her marriage, however, ended in divorce in 1969. Apparently undaunted, she married her second husband, Peter Duffy, in the same year, and again produced two children in quick succession and another critical work: *Wordsworth and Coleridge in their Time* (1970). In 1972 her son was killed by a drunk driver and Byatt shelved her third novel and took a full time lecturing post at University College, London.

When Byatt returned to the novel, the first in a projected quartet, she also returned to the thematic conflict between family life and the life of the mind. *The Virgin in the Garden* (1978) again focuses on two sisters: Frederica, a pert and precociously intelligent school girl, and Stephanie, her placid though brainy sister. It is set in the 1950s and the "desperation" Byatt writes of in her preface to *The Shadow of the Sun*, is embodied by Stephanie, who falls in love with a fat cleric and weeps over the inevitable consequences: "she had lost, or buried, a world in agreeing to marry" (p. 332). In the sequel, *Still Life* (1985), Stephanie attempts to recover that world, snatching a few desperate hours in the local library to think, and even trying to read Wordsworth through her ante-natal appointments, but her mental energy is sapped by her nascent family. The tragic conclusion to this novel is Stephanie's literal martyrdom to domesticity in the form of electrocution by an unearthed fridge.

Frederica, on the other hand, is a fully paid-up member of the "hungry generation." In *Still Life*, she panics when a girl in her college at Cambridge is sent down because she has got married: "In

1955 Frederica felt contempt, mixed with fear . . . surely, surely it was possible, she said to herself in a kind of panic, to make something of one's life *and* be a woman. Surely." But it is no coincidence that as a whey-faced, red-haired schoolgirl in *The Virgin in the Garden*, she is cast as Elizabeth I, the Virgin Queen, in a play written by Alexander Wedderburn (the love interest) for the second Elizabeth's coronation. The first Elizabeth famously refused to enter the human cycle of birth and death, rejecting love for political power, and Frederica unwittingly follows her lead. Having mercilessly pursued the recalcitrant Wedderburn, Frederica at the last minute evades the potential danger of sexual passion, choosing instead to divest herself of her hymen with clinical deliberation and keep her emotions and intellect intact.

The message in Byatt's fiction prior to *Possession* seems to be that women cannot have it all. However, as the action of her novels moves forwards, or backwards into the mythical time of fairy tale, Byatt betrays a cautious optimism as her female protagonists achieve qualified success or compromise between what have previously been presented as mutually exclusive states. When Byatt returns to the Frederica novels in 1996 with *Babel Tower*, Frederica has married incongruously and had a son, and is now trapped in a violent relationship and a "lady of the manor" role for which she has neither the talent nor the inclination. After escaping her Bluebeard's castle with a wounded thigh, venereal disease, and her young son, she embarks on a project of self-liberation through divorce and economic independence through work. At the same time she attempts to represent her experience in a series of "laminations" — a kind of narrative collage. At the end of the novel although she has won custody of her son and demonstrated her sexual liberation, the success of her emotional life is questionable. In spite of a tentative resolution to a romance in *Babel Tower*, when we see her next in "real" time in the prefatory chapter of *Still Life* (over ten years later), she is apparently unattached, though the projected sequel (provisionally entitled "A Whistling Woman"), may reveal otherwise.

The character who seems most likely to achieve the balance between professional and personal autonomy and romantic attachment is Maud at the end of *Possession*, when the novel predicts a "modern" solution to the female dilemma. This apparent reconciliation could be ascribed to the dictates of the romance genre, but it appears to be based on personal observation of social trends. As Byatt writes in her 1991 preface to *The Shadow of the Sun*: "I meet women now who work in different places from their husbands, and meet at weekends, to talk, and I envy them what I believe to be their certainty that they have a right to this." The reconciliation of the personal/professional dilemma can be ascribed to two related circumstances: broader society has caught up with early feminism so that the problem itself is no longer so acute; and the conflict no longer impinges directly or in the same way on Byatt's own life. Her children have grown up and, according to journalist Mira Stout, her husband gets his own dinner. *The Matisse Stories* (1993), concern the plight of middle-aged women, but demonstrate the same qualified optimism as the later novels.

Byatt is increasingly interested in witches, post-menopausal women who possess magic (creative) powers but may be made scapegoats by those who fear that power. The precursor of these figures is Winifred Potter, Stephanie and Frederica's mother in *Still Life*, who is quietly raging against family life and is described in the physical and emotional throes of the menopause as "an old witch in agony on her pyre" (p. 148). Winifred is a victim of family life and social expectations but lacks the resources to address her situation. "The Dried Witch" in *Sugar and Other Stories* (1987) equips herself with magic powers, but is punished by being tied to a tree and left to perish in the burning sun. Although Byatt now often identifies herself with the witch, for her the condition is one of liberation. In an interview she uses the metaphor of fire to describe a state of creative power experienced during a period of solitude at her house in the South of France: "I found myself alone in this house, and there was total silence, and the sun was absolutely blazing, and I walked up and down the stairs absolutely boiling with the sense that I belonged to myself, and could finish any thought."

THE ARTIST AND THE CRITIC

In addition to a thematic play between female creativity and domesticity, there is a thematic opposition set up between the artist and the critic, which similarly moves towards resolution in *Possession*'s Roland Michell, for whom professional success as a literary researcher and a poetic voice are achieved at the same time. Byatt's own career appears to have combined critical and creative writing from the first, and she asserts in *On Histories and Stories*: "I have myself always felt that reading and writing and teaching were all part of some whole that it was dangerous to disintegrate." But it is clear that she identifies herself as a "writer," emphasizing her literary skills over her academic credentials to journalists: "I am *not* an academic who happens to have written a novel. I am a novelist who happens to be quite good academically." Her novels have fairly regularly been followed by works of non-fiction, but as her fiction has become more self-conscious in its discussion of literature itself, her non-fiction has moved from the conventional studies of major writers penned by a professional academic, to eclectic collections of essays which demonstrate particular writerly preoccupations.

In the novels, the artist and the critic are often antagonistic and there is the same tendency to privilege the creative over the critical. Byatt asserts the primary importance of literature and the parasitical nature of criticism in her first novel. Henry Severell, who is based on the literary mystic D. H. Lawrence, though not an entirely sympathetic character, represented for Byatt the desire for what "I felt we [women] perhaps ought not to want, singlemindedness, art, vision." It is, she writes in the preface, "about the secondary imagination feeding off, and taming, the primary." Oliver the critic is based on F. R. Leavis, the pugnacious, authoritative don who held court at Cambridge in both Byatt's and her mother's time and has influenced generations of literary critics. Oliver can only reflect the light of Henry Severell's blinding talent—he is a hanger-on. The novel also dramatizes the potential antagonism between the artist and the critic; it is "about the paradox of Leavis preaching Lawrence when if the two had ever met they would have hated each other." Oliver's seduction of Anna can be read as a repulsive attempt to possess something that Henry has created. Although Byatt's feelings for Lawrence are ambivalent, her Cambridge experience appears to have calcified a suspicion of dogmatic intellectual authority, and spawned a particular antipathy to Leavis. He is held responsible for the quashing of Blackadder's creative impulses in *Possession*. There is an academic poet, Raphael Faber, in *Still Life*, who suggests the possibility of the two forms of writing co-existing, but he is a fairly minor character (straight out of Iris Murdoch's world), another recalcitrant male for Frederica to pursue.

In spite of various teaching posts and the publication of conventional critical work, Byatt's attitude to academia and the discourses it spawns remains ambivalent. She took the first step on the road to professional academia by going on to postgraduate work, but she was discouraged from completing her Ph.D. by the withdrawal of her grant. Furthermore, her supervisor at Oxford, the distinguished critic Helen Gardner, actively discouraged her novel writing and although she taught for over twenty years, she appears to have found students "selfish" and uninspiring. Byatt now has distinct reservations about the state of contemporary literary scholarship, which she has addressed in recent novels. Introduced to structuralist theory in the 1960s, Byatt has come to see the view of language as a self-enclosed system that it perpetrates as positively dangerous and writes in *Passions of the Mind* : "I am afraid of, and fascinated by, theories of language as a self-referring system of signs, which doesn't touch the world. I am afraid of, and resistant to, artistic stances which say we explore only our own subjectivity." Critical of these ways of thinking, she manages both to express her skepticism and demonstrate her mastery of such esoteric ideas in her novels. In *Possession*, she corrects and sometimes derogates post structuralist excesses, by parodying its jargon and revealing its potential to produce misreadings. Roland effectively grows out of structuralism when he finds his poetic voice. Phineas G. Nanson, the protagonist of *The Biographer's Tale*, rejects the theoretical orthodoxy of structuralism for the more fruitful uncertainties of biographical research. But in spite of the possibility of reconciling primary and secondary imagination — even though Roland has found his voice, he will still be employed as a critic — Leavis is never forgiven and the academy is a place whose intellectual doctrines suppress true intellectual freedom.

Byatt was out of the Academy when she wrote in the preface to the 1994 edition of *Degrees of Freedom*:

The nature of criticism has changed a great deal. . . . Critics have become very professional, politicised and relatively powerful, and writers have lost authority. As this happens, what writers write about writing seems almost to be a genre of its own, almost the only place where the kind of delighted reading I did when I first discovered Iris Murdoch can, in public, go on.

At this point Byatt had already published *Passions of the Mind*, a collection of essays on writers she admired, and has subsequently gone on to publish more writings about writing with *Imagining Characters* and *On Histories and Stories*. These eclectic collections of essays, in which Byatt displays her "delighted reading," were published at the point where she had established herself as an authority, but had no professional need to follow academic trends.

ROMANCE AND REALISM

British fiction, particularly the mainstream "woman's novel" has historically been associated with literary realism rather than the experimentalism of avant-garde "high" art. Byatt's fiction follows a trajectory, which leads her away from literary realism towards a self-conscious and experimental postmodernism. However, Byatt has referred to herself as a "self-conscious realist," and from the first her novels have explored the theme of artistic representation, often via a character's struggles with some form of artistic creation or self-expression, so that technique — imagery and language — becomes topic. As her postmodernist self-consciousness develops, the authorial-narratorial voice becomes less dependent on the central character's experience and train of thought and discourses at length directly with the reader in a mode known as "intrusive narration." This technique is practically as old as the novel itself and was practiced by major eighteenth-century novelists such as Henry Fielding.

As a well-educated young writer, Byatt had plenty of literary role models; however contemporary female writers of any stature were thin on the ground. She found the male model unappealing: the "Angry Young Men," a high-profile group christened by the media, in extreme reaction to the techniques and literary sensibility of modernism, were a rather aggressive and misogynistic lot. Byatt alludes to this group in *The Virgin in the Garden* as the producers of "threadbare 'satire', a sluggish and ponderous anti-rhetoric, a laboured passion for deflating almost anything" (p. 318), although she, like them, finds unappealing the feminine sensibility of the most influential female modernist, Virginia Woolf. In *The Shadow of the Sun* she acknowledges a structural debt to Elizabeth Bowen and Rosamond Lehmann, novelists who started writing at the tail end of modernism but were still publishing in the 1960s, and also cites the stylistic influence of the contemporary French novelist Francoise Sagan's *Bonjour Tristesse*. She also mentions that she had read Proust and discovered Iris Murdoch, "both of whom combine a kind of toughness of thought with a sensuous awareness," between the first and second drafts of the novel. The link with Murdoch, which is sustained in later novels, is both in the subject of Anna's existential dilemma and the literary execution. The dialogue and narration of the story are fairly conventional, sometimes pedestrian; there is an impersonal third-person narrator, but also an attention to the physical world—the "sensuality" of which Byatt speaks—which Murdoch relates to a moral state, and which Byatt associates with Anna's artistic vision.

What is most significant in the first novel in terms of the development of Byatt's literary "voice" is the use of imagery and symbolism. Byatt writes in her preface about her perennial theme: female (and male) creativity in terms of light imagery, sun, and moon. Henry is associated with the sun, and in his state of visionary ecstasy, attains his own luminescent and incandescent power. Anna, who like Oliver manages only a feeble reflection, has her own moment of illumination at night in a thunderstorm. This passage in which the reader sees what Anna sees is typical of Byatt in high literary mode, and is characterized by a combination of unconventional diction and related, repeated images:

The shelves were a miracle of green and silver, shadow of transparent shadow, reflected and admitted, block geometry made ideal in light, under the brittle circular shadows of the glasses, which rested on them and through them. Shadows of light, Anna thought, thickness on thickness, all these textures of light, caught and held in glass, spirals and cones and pencil trellises, where the shadow of one shelf overlapped another. (p. 133)

Although this is all seen through Anna's eyes, we are effectively removed from the action to dwell on Anna's fitful vision. She thinks: "I can do something with this, that matters," though in the end the vision fails. The same kind of imagery is also used extensively in *The Virgin in the Garden*, where the disturbed adolescent, Marcus, is plagued by visions of light and a fearful perception of the world in terms of a threatening and animated geometry. Marcus's creative powers are later turned towards the sciences rather than the arts.

Byatt has increasingly elevated herself above the mainstream of post-war women's fiction by producing novels which were dominated by an intellectual conceit, and a self-consciousness of their own literary devices and construction—one of the trademarks of postmodern fiction. She describes her second novel *The Game* as a technical exercise in metaphor, and it is heavily peppered with symbol, marking the introduction of Byatt's preoccupation with the natural sciences, in this case dramatized through the herpetologist love interest, Simon. *The Game* is still by and large a conventional, story-driven novel. Byatt's self-conscious literariness really starts to come into play with *The Virgin in the Garden*. In this novel the central event, the play, allows for repeated reference to literary conceits and a historical parallel is drawn between the first Elizabethan age and 1950s Britain. Here and in the subsequent novel there is a degree of naturalization in that much of the narrative commentary is prompted by the consciousness of the highly literate characters Stephanie, Frederica, and Alexander. But Byatt often moves from a character's thought process or internal monologue to a more intrusive narrative commentary and back again. Just before Stephanie is shown weeping at the thought of her forthcoming marriage, she has been thinking about language and literature. At one point the author-narrator leaves off simply recounting Stephanie's thought process to address the reader directly:

A passion for reading . . . can be hinted but not told out, since to describe an impassioned reading of [Wordsworth's] *Books* would take many more pages that *Books* itself and be an anticlimax. Nor is it possible like Borges' poet, to incorporate *Books* into this text, though the fear of the drowning of books and its determination to give a fictive substance to a figure seen in a dream might lend a kind of Wordsworthian force to the narrative. (pp. 331–332)

This complicated passage, though motivated by Stephanie's preoccupation with her soon-to-be-married state, exists primarily as a vehicle for Byatt to address her current theoretical and practical preoccupations as a writer.

The central metaphor of *Still Life* is taken from the visual arts, specifically the post-impressionist work of Vincent van Gogh. As well as continuing to dramatize the lives and loves of its protagonists, motivated in this by Alexander's work in progress on the artist, the novel frequently focuses on techniques of representation using painterly metaphors. Again, having discussed specific narrative events, the narrator often proceeds to address related matters at a higher level of abstraction. After an account of Stephanie's infant son and his blurred sight and speculation on how the child might verbalize this vision, the narrator discourses on art and alludes to the writing of the novel itself:

Art is not the recovery of the innocent eye, which is inaccessible. "Make it new" cannot mean, see it free of all learned frames and names, for paradoxically it is only a precise use of learned comparison and the signs we have made to distinguish things seen or recognised that can give the illusion of newness. I had the idea that this novel could be written innocently, without recourse to reference to other people's thoughts, without, as far as possible, recourse to simile or metaphor. This turned out to be impossible[.] (108)

Byatt's novel does not merely utilize simile and metaphor, it is about these literary figures. The quoted passage moves towards metafiction proper: reference to the fictional status of the text. Readers may become irritated when the action is too often or too lengthily inter-rupted by an intrusive narrator bent on discussing issues at a more abstract level, but Byatt's narrator leads us quite gently in and out of the metafictional mode, which arguably helps to sustain the fictional illusion.

Byatt is often, and with reason, called an intellectual writer, indeed the "cleverness" of the novels is something which often appears to irritate even reviewers in the more literary journals. Byatt herself is rather impatient with those who cavil at the intellectualism of her novels and in an interview rejects the implication that it is somehow inappropriate for a woman novelist:

I am still baffled slightly by the reaction to my mixture of ideas and sensuality. I also think it's one of the places where I do feel faintly feminist. I don't think people get so angry with men for having ideas and sensuality, in quite the same way. Nobody shouts at Tolstoy that he didn't understand sex because he spent a lot of time thinking metaphysically about the nature of the universe and the nature of philosophy.

Comparison with Murdoch is again relevant. Murdoch is known for her commitment to a kind of realism, which specifies paying attention to things (what Byatt calls "sensuality"), but she has also been called a "metaphysical" novelist, suggesting the intellectual underpinning of her work. Richard Todd, who has written on both authors, distinguishes between their respective fictional worlds. They both work from or with the realist tradition, deliberately bending, stretching and corrupting it by incorporating intellectual and metafictional elements. However, Byatt's social world in *The Virgin in the Garden* and *Still Life* is more ordinary, more grounded in the everyday, and in this sense better realized than Murdoch's somewhat stylized representation of the bohemian, bourgeois, or intellectual middle classes.

Byatt retains the commitment to imaginative realization and sensual description, but domestic realism has progressively dissipated as the author has encountered and been influenced by other literatures and histories. Byatt has latterly described herself as moving away from the British model and states in *On Histories and Stories* that she sees herself increasingly as a "European writer." European postmodernism, typified in the work of Umberto Eco, Italo Calvino or Jorge Luis Borges (the latter South American), is not afraid of parading its literariness. British readers are less accustomed to intellectual or "idea-led" fiction, which may inform Byatt's assertion:

Most novel readers don't look in novels for the kind of thoughts they have when thinking about their work. The just look to be able to relax into a world of personal relationships. [. . .] I'm actually creating a kind of whole which contains thinking and feeling all at once. This is annoying for people whose lives are compartmentalised: they do their thinking and then they come home and do their feeling. And their novel reading is part of their feeling life.

Byatt's novels have always been underpinned by an intellectual scheme and from the first have been obviously *literary* works of fiction. While the later fiction still deals with the themes of domesticity, creativity, and female autonomy, it explores them through such diverse, complex, and self-consciously literary means that the form becomes more prominent and militates against the aura of ordinariness which characterizes literary realism. Her latest novel *The Biographer's Tale* (2000), a relatively slim offering with her first male narrator, is described in the publicity as "Borges-like" and by the author as a "patchwork, echoing book." Its protagonist, Phineas K. Nanson, gives up literary theory in favor of biographical research into Scholes Destry-Scholes, himself a biographer of bigamist Victorian poet and polymath, Elmer Bole. As in *Possession*, events in Phineas's life are paralleled by those of his biographical subjects, not least in his involvement with two distinctively different women. Subtitled, "A Novel," realism here is attenuated not so much by the inset texts and historical parallels as by the peculiar names and strange affairs of the characters in the main narrative. There is a partial trajectory discernible in Byatt's work, which in terms of form commences with domestic realism and literariness combined, gradually shifts into the idea-led but imaginatively realized fictional world of *Possession*, and in this last novel approaches anti-realist fabulation. At the same time the theme of female creativity and vision has been supplanted by a less gender-specific interest in dramatizing contemporary theories of knowledge.

Byatt has said in the interview that "The nice thing about a novel is that everything can go into it, because if you've got the skill between sentence and sentence, you can change genre, you can change focus, you can change the way the reader reads. And yet you can keep up this sort of quiet momentum of narration." Her later novels incorporate more and more by way of literary device and formal variety. *Babel Tower* incorporates substantial quotations of various kinds: trial transcripts, extracts from "real" novels, fictional children's stories, and Frederica's "laminations." Most significantly, the novel contains extracts from *Babbletower*, an allegory of 1960s libertarian ideology taken to its obscene extreme. *Babbletower* is eventually naturalized and incorporated within the present action of *Babel Tower* when it emerges that it has been written by one of the characters. *Possession* is the most varied and inclusive book in Byatt's oeuvre and it is hard to conceive that a novel could contain much more without sacrificing the readerly appeal that made it such a spectacular success.

2

The Novel

A POSTMODERN ROMANCE

Possession is subtitled "A Romance," a label which might at first glance suggest a simple love story. A romance in the most basic sense is a narrative whose plot is driven by the initial attraction and subsequent obstacles two lovers have to overcome in order to progress towards the inevitable happy union. It does not take the reader long to realize that this novel is no such thing, that it contains not one, but two love stories — one contemporary and one Victorian — whose plots are intertwined. In addition, these stories are studded with other narratives and texts: poems and fairy tales; extracts from biography and criticism; letters and diaries. Byatt, by temperament and in principle, resists the restrictions of categorization, complaining in *On Histories and Stories* that contemporary "Novels are taught if they appear to have something to contribute to the debate about 'women's writing' or 'feminism' or 'post-colonial studies' or 'postmodernism'." Critics and theorists have also made much of the difficulties of defining postmodernism and it is true that one cannot satisfactorily analyze a novel by slapping a convenient label on it, but *Possession* bears many of the hallmarks of a contemporary postmodern novel, one of which is a kind of "pick-and-mix" approach to genre. Postmodern fiction often disrupts hierarchies of genre, by incorporating elements from or alluding to both popular genres and historically more elevated forms. *Possession* can also be categorized as a "historiographic metafiction," a postmodern genre which addresses history as a constructed narrative, a *story*, whose claim to truth-telling is questionable. To this end, in Byatt's words:

Possession plays serious games with the variety of possible forms of narrating the past—the detective story, the biography, the mediaeval verse Romance, the modern romantic novel, and Hawthorne's fantastic historical Romance in between, the campus novel, the Victorian third-person narration, the epistolary novel, the forged manuscript novel, and the primitive fairy tale . . .

The novel also characteristically plays with established narrative conventions when character or narrator reminds the reader that s/he is reading a work of fiction by musing on the nature of fictional representation itself.

HOW TO READ THE NOVEL

Byatt is playing intellectual games in a novel which is stuffed full of literary allusion. The novel is informed by a lifetime's reading and some specific scholarly research. The very names of the contemporary hero and heroine contain a wealth of literary allusion, some of which is flagged in the text, and some of which is less obvious. That Maud is connected with Tennyson's Maud, for example, is flagged in the repeated quotation "icily regular, splendidly null," and further suggested by the fact that *Possession*'s Maud works at the top of Tennyson Tower. The name Roland refers back to the medieval French *Chanson de Roland*, whose hero is betrothed to the homophonic Aude and to Browning's "Childe Roland to the Dark Tower Came", and hence linked to the "Childe" in Christabel's story "The Threshold." There are so many allusions to other (real) literary texts in the novel that it is not possible to gloss them in this study. In the final paragraph of Chapter 15, for example, Christabel mentions George Herbert, the seventeenth-century Metaphysical poet and quotes in the original from Goethe's *Faust*. Ash responds by quoting two lines from Andrew Marvell's "To His Coy Mistress," without citing author or title. All of these have reference to the couple's situation: Faust in Goethe's play is tempted by the devil with sensual pleasures, and at risk of losing his soul if he cries out: "Stay, thou art so fair." "To His Coy Mistress" is a *Carpe Diem* poem, a genre in which the poetic speaker attempts to persuade his mistress to enjoy the pleasures of the flesh today rather than worrying about tomorrow. George Herbert wrote on the struggle between earthly delight and heavenly love (see "The Agonie").

Rather than asking how such a novel may be interpreted, it may initially be instructive to think about how such a dense, complex, intellectual, allusive, novel may be *read*. Byatt has said, on more than one occasion, that she expects readers to "skip" bits in her novels: "I have always known that a wise writer should understand that all readers skip, and will skip. I think, unfortunately, most readers skip most quotations these days, thinking wrongly that they know them or ought to, already. It isn't so." *Possession* might seem to court this practice because of devices such as intercutting the parallel plot with substantial "other" texts: poetry, biography, diary and journal, so that the main parallel plot lines—the romance between the two couples, and the discovery of this romance—are disrupted and interrupted. These are relevant to the main plot but disrupt and retard the action.

No one can tell a recreational reader how to read; no doubt many have been put off, as even some critics have, by the degree of erudition in the novel. Byatt may see reading, criticism, and writing as a continuum, rather than a set of discrete activities, but whereas a recreational reader can "skip" with impunity, a critic must diligently plod through. The reader does not necessarily have to recognize every allusion or have an intimate knowledge of the lives and works of the real Victorian poets on whom Christabel and Randolph Henry Ash are at least partially modeled, to appreciate the fictional poetry and to link the content of that poetry with the fictional lives. On the other hand, the literary allusions are not arbitrary; they often say something about character through connotation, "deepening" the meaning and reinforcing the links between parallel romances and inset texts. What makes the novel a particularly artful literary object and rewards the assiduous reader is the way that the epigraphs, quotations, and inset texts echo and are interwoven with the main narrative strands, making the novel both complex and coherent, multi-layered but unified.

As the main title suggests, the novel is about possession, and in line with its complex form dramatizes multiple aspects of this theme, exploring the nature of possessive love and the contrary impulse to self-preservation; superficial possession — of things — and supernatural possession by ghosts, literal and metaphorical; the quest for knowledge (intellectual possession) against the capacity of literary texts to exceed interpretation and of historical events to evade attempts to uncover them. The novel also argues, implicitly, for the superiority of fiction in revealing a kind of truth over criticism, biography, or history, whose access to facts is always only partial. The way that the novel is constructed reinforces in particular this last message and the remainder of this section of the Guide will explore the various aspects of theme and form and analyze their relation within the novel.

Love and Romance

The story starts with Roland Michell's acquisition of two drafts of a letter from Randolph Henry Ash to an unknown woman. In spite of his usually law-abiding temperament, Roland is "seized by a strange and uncharacteristic impulse" to steal these mysterious letters and thus the quest narrative, whose holy grail is knowledge, is introduced. Gripped by a mounting sense of excitement, Roland's pursuit of the answer to this mystery leads him first to undertake his own research, tentatively identifying the unnamed addressee as minor poet Christabel LaMotte, then to seek out the "redoubtable" Maud as an expert on LaMotte. Maud, who finds the mystery equally compelling, becomes both his accomplice in this quest, and object of the romance narrative which is instituted at the same time. This contemporary love story runs parallel with and is formally interwoven with the story of the Victorian lovers as the modern academics' quest for knowledge of the past drives the postmodern romance.

Passionate love is conventionally described as a kind of madness, a heightened state of mind and body in which the subject's whole being is possessed by the loved one. It can also be marked by the desperate desire to possess the other person. But the postmodern lovers have an intellectual suspicion of the very idea of love: "They were children of a time and culture which mistrusted love, 'in love', romantic love, romance *in toto*" (p. 423). Their quest to uncover the Victorian's romance involves them, in a double sense, in a romance narrative. In the library at Seal Court, in spite of a frosty atmosphere and a frosty Maud, Roland's disappointed vision of a shared intellectual project, made possible by the discovery of the "dolly" letters, signals the romantic potential of the partnership, which is confirmed by the electric shocks which pass between the couple first at the pond and again as Maud emerges, all silky and wet, from the bathroom. Each time, they retire. For most of the novel's action, Roland and Maud are more eager to satisfy their narrative curiosity than any libidinous urges because they have a particular fear of romantic entanglement: Roland because of his claustrophobic and moribund relationship with the droopy and sullen Val, from which he is weedily unable to extricate himself; Maud because of an equally claustrophobic affair with the glamorous Fergus, which returns in repeated flashbacks of a rumpled bed like "whipped-up dirty egg white," a contrast to Christabel's riddling image of the inviolable egg in her letter to Ash.

Part of Roland and Maud's mutual attraction is, paradoxically, a shared desire for solitude. It emerges that they both have a vision of a solitary white bed. The couple is highly resistant to any aspect of love, including sexual involvement, which threatens autonomy, hence the tentative progress of their romance. The problem with excessive self-possession is that it makes difficult the giving of oneself that is part of the idea of romantic love. There are various physical symbols which suggest Maud's effort of self-restraint, including the pristine neatness of her flat, and more significantly the confinement of her hair — a conventional symbol of sexual availability or license. She does, however, more than Christabel, see this resistance as a problem, a lack, asking herself: "Why could she do nothing with ease and grace except work alone, inside these walls and curtains, her bright safe box?" (pp. 136–37). Even in France when their trip takes on a honeymooning aspect and they join each other in a white bed: "They took to silence. They touched each other without comment and without progression" (p. 423). But the romance progresses in spite of their hang-ups, driven by the narrative of the braver and more innocent Victorians.

The Victorian love affair is characterized by its passionate intensity. Randolph Henry Ash appears to have an inbuilt predilection for the state of being possessed. In his courtship letter to Ellen, he has written that his *"most ardent desire is to be* possessed entirely *by thoughts of you"* (p. 460), but he is significantly signaling his failure to achieve this exalted state. In his attraction to Christabel he achieves the desired condition: "For months he had been possessed by the imagination of her" (pp. 276–77). Christabel's initial resistance and desire for solitude is overcome by his epistolary wooing. Her objection to the relationship seems not initially to be a conventional rejection of adultery in Victorian society, but rather a deliberate rejection of love and romance in favor of a well-regulated exclusively female domestic set-up in which artistic creation was made possible. Christabel clearly values both this effortfully constructed life and the degree of autonomy it allows her, hence her reluctance to become involved with Ash. She writes to Ash that even their letter writing could compromise her reputation in the eyes of the world and thus imperil her freedom, but is moved to meet him in Richmond Park by Blanche Glover's efforts to squash the nascent affair. Thereafter her letters protest the threat to her autonomy, and his continue to importune. When he overcomes her resistance and their epistolary courtship develops into a full-blown, if clandestine, affair, it is striking that Ash displays a stereotypical masculine romanticism, more content to live in the present, possessed of the moment; whereas even during their first night together Christabel cannot forget the practical implications of their liaison and the future—presciently as it turns out. Although she "gives" herself to Ash — a daring and ultimately costly move in the context of Victorian social and sexual mores — she retains a degree of self-possession (pride) which enables her to reject and evade Ash, even though she is pregnant with his child.

The reader does not witness the end of the affair and is party to its aftermath, with Roland and Maud, through Sabine's journal. It appears from Ash's later letter that he has only been constrained to let her go because he is unable to find her when she flees to Brittany to await the delivery of her child. At one point in the novel, Ash considers the way to win Christabel: "He would teach her that she was not his possession" (p. 279). In fact she teaches him this lesson when she flees the country. It is at this point — his forcible dispossession of Christabel, a separation executed primarily through her strength of will — that romantic love starts to take on the aspect of supernatural possession, a more frightening and repellent condition in which the subject is unwillingly or forcibly inhabited by the other: "A possession, as by daemons" is how Ash describes his love for Christabel to Ellen. This is further emphasized by his violent reaction at the séance of Hella Lees at which Christabel is also present; skeptical Ash is tormented by not knowing whether his child has lived or died. After the birth of her child by Ash, Christabel manages to claw back some of her self-possession, or at least a kind of solitude, but at the cost of giving up her daughter and the emotional torture of physical proximity with the child who does not know its mother. She and Ash remain linked in their lifetimes, poignantly, through this child, whom neither of them can publicly own.

The trajectory of Maud and Roland's affair is slower, but they overcome their native or acquired caution, even to the extent of admitting to an all consuming love: "All the things we — we grew up not believing in. Total obsession, night and day" (p. 506). The arrangement that Roland proposes at the end of the novel, "a modern way," is for him to take a job abroad and leave Maud, at least part of the time, to her work and herself, a solution to their mutual need for autonomy and love. Thus the end of the novel at least potentially resolves the tension between passion and self-possession.

BIOGRAPHY

Literary biography—the activity of researching another person's life and work—incorporates an analogous double aspect of possession. The biographer desires to possess his or her subject through an exhaustive knowledge, and at the same time this obsession with the subject may come to possess the biographer. This idea of the dual aspect of biography impinged on Byatt and provided the germ of *Possession*, while she was herself writing a conventional work of biographical criticism, *Wordsworth and Coleridge in their Time* (1970). In the course of her work, she came across the Coleridge scholar Kathleen Coburn, who had been working on her subject for thirty years and reported later in an interview:

It came to me that possession worked both ways—she thought Coleridge's thoughts and his thoughts were entirely mediated by her. Then much later I got the ideas of the spiritualist mediums, possession in that sense, and sexual possession, if you had two poets rather than one, and economic possession.

The relationship between the literary subject and biographer is presented as somewhat unhealthy—the biographer loses her own identity yet imposes herself between Coleridge and the reader. Whereas love provisionally conquers all in the postmodern romance, literary biography, which imposes the biographer's interpretation on the life and work of dead subject, remains simply provisional.

When asked whether she had ever been tempted by biography, Byatt replies in the negative citing the reason as:

a primitive fear of possession. I do not wish to spend most of my life on somebody else's life—not one other person's life.

The words came to me long before the plot of the novel, *Possession*, and it was to do with being taken over—or alternatively, taking somebody over, depending on whether you're a sympathiser or a hunter.

This distinction between "hunter" and "sympathiser" is one that pertains to the literary critics in the novel. The hunters include Cropper, Fergus, and Leonora; the sympathizers are Roland, Maud, and Beatrice Nest.

Roland can be directly contrasted to the biographer and custodian Mortimer Cropper, whose business it is to acquire the effects of Ash and who pursues this business with single-minded zeal. Although Cropper's psychological motivation is complex, his acquisitive nature is clear. It emerges through his projected autobiography that he is the descendent of collectors and that he regards his home as a kind of museum. We first see Cropper, an incongruously garbed figure, crouched on a lavatory seat in a suburban bathroom. He is also purloining a letter—or rather a copy of it—by equally underhand means, the difference being that his methods are carefully calculated and well practised. The means by which Cropper will obtain the smallest remnant of Ash are minutely calculated, but he is able to throw any amount of money after his goal. The way he puts it to his suburban hostess betrays a desire almost to *own* the man: "It is my aim to know as far as possible everything he did— everyone who mattered to him—every little preoccupation he had" (p. 96). Cropper's preoccupation with his subject is certainly unhealthy. Cropper's name, like many in the novel, tells us something about his character. The name "Cropper" incorporates "crop" or maw of a bird and could also connote reaper/raper. The man himself is a greedy and slightly sinister character, magpie-like accumulating the effects of Randolph Henry Ash, like his nice shiny watch. "Mortimer" incorporates an etymological element of death; he drives "a swift funereal car," has a penchant for black clothes, has turned the Stant Collection into a kind of mausoleum for Ash's effects. He is obsessed with a dead man to the extent of violating his grave.

Cropper's ironically titled biography, *The Great Ventriloquist*, betrays the man in that the voice and personality of the author are ironically obtrusive. His morbid obsession and maladjusted ego manifest themselves in this work, which Maud judges to be "as much about its author as its subject, and she did not find Mortimer Cropper's company pleasant" (p. 246). It is a form of self-aggrandizement: "He had a peculiarly vicious version of reverse hagiography; the desire to cut his subject down to size" (p. 250) and shore up his own ego. The narrator implies that he has a tenuous self-identity: "He tended his body, the outward man, with a fastidiousness that he would have bestowed on the inner man too, if he had known who he was" (p. 99). Although it is revealed in his lecture on "The Art of the Biographer" that Cropper, exploiting new technology, is as attached to reproductions, simulacra, of the things as much as the things himself, he owns Ash's watch, an object which he now keeps close to his chest: "For he believed the watch had come to him, that it had been meant to come to him, that he had and held something of R. H. Ash. It ticked near his heart. He would have liked to be a poet" (p. 387). These last two sentences, not grammatically connected, reveal Cropper's desire to *be* his subject, the ultimate form of possession, also desired by lovers.

Biography itself has long been regarded as a faintly populist and disreputable form of scholarship. Since the early twentieth century when English Literature was just establishing itself as a respectable academic subject, there has been a dominant idea in literary criticism that the only proper object of study is the literary text, and that the life of the author is largely irrelevant to this study, a view that Byatt has some sympathy with and both Roland and Maud appear to share. Although Roland initially tells his sulky girlfriend Val that his theft of Ash's letter may lead to better job prospects, his injured and flustered response to Maud's suggestion that the theft was motivated by profit reveals a more complex motive: "It was something *personal*. You wouldn't know. I'm an old-fashioned textual critic, not a biographer—I don't go in for this sort of—it wasn't *profit*—I'll put them back next week—I wanted them to be a secret. Private. And to do the work" (p. 50). For Roland the letter doesn't represent profit, though it does have monetary value and in the end does improve his career prospects, but mystery, a quest whose holy grail is knowledge. His identification with textual scholarship and distaste for biography is echoed by Maud on their visit to "Bethany": when she also asserts: "I'm a textual scholar" (p. 211). However, Roland and Maud, in their compelling desire to know more, become biographers in spite of themselves.

Maud, with her own fear of intimacy and intrusion respects the privacy of her subjects, and could not be accused of prurient interest. The fact remains that she has a great deal of natural sympathy with her subject, Christabel, because of the psychological similarities between the two: their desire to remain aloof from messy and potentially harmful involvements and commitment to their work. Roland's nature and physical appearance militate against identifying him as a hunter or a grabber. But as the action progresses, and Roland and Maud in turn are pursued by Leonora and Cropper, they become more and more devious in their methods. Maud effectively steals Sabine's diary from Leonora by intercepting Ariane LeMinier's letter, and by the end of the novel she and Roland are effectively accessories to a repellent crime — the grave-robbing episode. However it is emphasized in the novel that they are driven by *narrative* curiosity rather than the common or garden kind, the desire to know the end of the story for its own sake so the reader's sympathy with the twentieth-century biographers need not be compromised.

VICTORIAN/MODERN BIOGRAPHY

As well as distinguishing hunters from sympathisers, the novel contrasts Victorian and contemporary biography as well as other kinds of scholarly activity. In *The Biographer's Tale*, Phineas G. Nanson, the novice biographer, considers the nature of contemporary biography, whose readers, "the British chattering classes," would look for "loves, hatreds, rivalries and friendships." He compares this invasive and prurient attitude to "the Victorian conventions of respecting privacy and not speaking ill of the dead" (p. 15). In *Possession*, although the Victorians' objection to biographical invasion is clearly strong, the practices of biographers seem no less unprincipled. Beatrice Nest refers to Ellen Ash's "sharp comments . . . about contemporary biographical habits — rumminging in Dickens's desk before he was fairly buried and that sort of thing — the usual Victorian comments" (p. 219) in Ellen Ash's journal. Ellen conceives this journal as "both a defence against, and a bait for, the gathering of ghouls and vultures" (p. 462).

The real difference between Victorian and twentieth-century biographers is the unabashed interest taken in the sex life of the biographical subject by the latter. For this development Freud, for whom socially unacceptable desire could reveal itself in dreams or unintentionally in literary texts, can be blamed. Phineas Nanson explains how first-wave Freudian biographies:

made the assumption explicit or implicit, that the direction of a subject's libido (more particularly the unconscious and unacknowledged directions) is the single most important thing about his, or her, life. The second wave of psychoanalytic biography entails elaborate unmaskings of contrary and hidden senses and motivations, so that often the "real" story appears to be the exact opposite of the "apparent" story[.] (pp. 15–16)

Leonora Stern represents aspects of both first and second wave Freudianism: she regards Christabel's sexuality as the single most important factor in her poetry and refuses to take Ellen Ash's journal at face value, assuming that the omissions sensed by Beatrice mask some secret about her sex life. While Leonora labours under a misapprehension in the first case, she is nearer the truth in the second. Ellen, it emerges, suffers from a psycho-sexual dysfunction which means that the Ashes' marriage is never consummated, a truly shocking state of affairs to a post-Freudian sensibility. However, this fact is revealed to the reader through Byatt's narrative method, but never available to the twentieth-century critics. Because of the way that this scene is dramatized, through Ellen's train of thought, it is one of the most shocking and pitiful scenes in the book. We learn of it first through Ellen's memories of her honeymoon in Chapter 25, the idyllic setting and the horror of the events: "A running creature, crouching and cowering in the corner of the room, its teeth chattering, its veins clamped in spasms, its breath shallow and fluttering. Herself." Her revulsion from and repulsion of her husband, "Not once, but over and over and over" (p. 459).

This technique, a kind of dramatic irony whereby the reader is party to knowledge of which the contemporary characters remain ignorant, is the prime means by which the novel demonstrates the slippery and provisional nature of biographical-historical knowledge. Roland and Maud's quest involves them ducking out of their strictly professional roles but in spite of their maverick approach to research, some things of significance remain uncovered. It is notable, however, that all those engaged in more orthodox scholarly activity prove even less well equipped to get at the truth and in this incompetence lies both the campus comedy and a serious attack on the shortcomings of modern academia. The aridity of academic work is represented by the hellish "Ash Factory" and its manager, Blackadder, who works in a smell of "metal, dust, metal-dust and burning plastic," and the images associated with Blackadder himself signify desolation and desiccation; he "was a grey man, with a grey skin and iron-grey hair. . . . His clothes, tweed jacket, cord trousers, were respectable, well-worn and dusty, like everything else down there" (pp. 29–30). Blackadder is one of those scholars who is possessed by his subject, but in his case, it is less a demonic possession than a rather dreary enslavement:

There were times when Blackadder allowed himself to see clearly that he would end his working life, that was to say his conscious thinking life, in this task, that all his thoughts would have been another man's thoughts, all his work another man's work. And then he thought it did not perhaps matter so greatly. He did after all find Ash fascinating, even after all these years. It was a pleasant subordination, if he was a subordinate. (p. 29)

The essentially secondary nature of Blackadder's work is clear; he is, like Cropper, a poet manqué, whose creative impulses have been stifled. At one point thinks about his work in terms of the metaphor of a naturalist analysing owl droppings: "He was pleased with this image and momentarily considered making a poem out of it. Then he discovered Ash had been beforehand with him." (p. 29) The Ash

Factory suggests the production of so much waste material and Blackadder's research results primarily in exponentially proliferating footnotes, which "engulfed and swallowed the text" (p. 28). His scholarly method, furthermore, is primarily one of negation: "Much of his time was spent deciding whether or not to erase things. He usually did." (p. 300)

Beatrice Nest is another tired and dispirited scholar, engaged in what is to her the promethean task of editing Ellen Ash's journals. Beatrice represents a professionally marginalized generation of women, pushed into a specialization thought to be suitable to her sex by the male-dominated institution of the time, but against her inclinations. Although she is associated with ovine imagery in Cropper's mind and there is a certain woolly quality to her character, her name and physical appearance also suggest a mother-hen, protectively sitting on Ellen's journal as on a cluster of eggs that is never going to hatch. Beatrice, a sympathizer rather than a hunter, is both incapable and unwilling to delve too deep into these journals out of respect for their author. She tells Maud: "You will think I am mad. I am trying to excuse twenty-five years' delay — with — personalities — You would have produced an edition twenty years ago. The truth is also, I wasn't sure it was right. If she would have liked what I was doing" (p. 221). Beatrice's intuitive reading is correct; she is professionally unsuccessful partly because of a sympathy for her subject and sensitivity to Ellen's unstated intention in her journal, an unwillingness to pry into what is not written, though unwittingly nearer the truth than those who have no compunction about intruding into the Victorians' private lives.

The bright young things of the academic world, it emerges, are little better equipped to get at the truth because they are blinkered by postmodern theory and slavish adherents to the post-Freudian criticism, which focuses on sex at the expense of the literary text.

Leonora is an arch-exponent of this kind of criticism, parodied in her essay on Christabel's *Melusine* in which each image is read as a symbol of female sexuality:

Melusine's fountain has a *female* wetness, trickling out from its pool rather than rising confidently, thus mirroring those female secretions which are not inscribed in our daily use of language (*langue*, tongue)—the sputum, mucus, milk and bodily fluids of women who are silent for dryness. (p. 245)

After Roland has read Leonora's rude essay, he complains "it all reduced like boiling jam to—human sexuality. Just as Leonora Stern makes the whole earth read as the female body—and language—all language. And all vegetation is pubic hair" (p. 253). As Roland suggests, Leonora's whole area of intellectual enquiry is motivated by and focused on lesbian sexuality and, it transpires, is based on at least a partial misapprehension regarding Christabel's sexuality, which in turn is the product of her own sexual predilections. It emerges that although Maud is influenced by contemporary feminist theory, and for a while labors under similar misapprehensions, she is not without some resistance to its all-encompassing claims. In response to Beatrice's objections to Leonora's approach, Maud replies: "Unfortunately feminism can hardly avoid privileging such matters. I sometimes wish I had embarked on geology myself."(p. 222), thus implicitly linking herself with the polymath Ash, and again endorsing the reader's sympathy. This message is reiterated on the visit to "Bethany" when she again "deplore[s] the modern feminist attitude to private lives" and avers: "You can be psychoanalytic without being *personal*" (p. 211). Both dyed-in-the-wool literary theorists are "hunters." The vulpine Fergus, with his "voracious smile" and "long mouth terribly full of strong white teeth," has taken Roland's job and mercilessly pursued and hectored Maud. Leonora is equally sexually predatory, though much cruder. Having worked her way through two husbands and a series of female lovers, she makes a wholly unwanted pass at Maud at her flat, attempting seduction by smothering, ignoring her heartfelt protests and violating her precious self-possession. The reader is led to sympathize with the repressed and prudish Roland and Maud, battling against an academic world which is sex-mad and theory-ridden.

The eclectic Victorian mind also comes off well against these modern obsessions. Byatt's stated intentions in writing a "historical" novel were "to do with rescuing the complicated Victorian thinkers from modern diminishing parodies like those of Fowles and Lytton Strachey." In an interview she puts the case for the Victorians and against literary theorists thus:

For the Victorians, everything was part of one thing: science, religion, philosophy, economics, politics, women, fiction, poetry. They didn't com-partmentalize—they thought BIG. Ruskin went out and learned geology and archaeology, then the history of painting, then mythology, and then he thought out, and he thought out. Now, if you get a literary theorist, they only talk to other literary theorists about literary theory. Nothing causes them to look out!

The Victorian scholar—polymath—is highly congenial to Byatt, whereas she objects particularly to the self-contained nature of struc-turalist and post-structuralist thought, which is based on an influential linguistic theory whose focus of interest was the relationship between words rather than the relationship between words and things in the world. Ash is precisely interested both in things in the world, as his pudding dishes full of specimens witness, and in words, and in the relationship between the two, dramatized in *The Garden of Proserpina*. Ash has a voracious mind which ranges over the arts and the sciences and combines meticulous observation with poetic

creation. As Blackadder observes, he "had been interested in everything. Arab astronomy and African transport systems, angels and
oakapples, hydraulics and the guillotine, druids, and the grande
armée, catharists and printers' devils, ectoplasm and solar mythology, the last meals of frozen mastodons and the true nature of
manna" (p. 28). In a letter to Ellen from his clandestine Yorkshire
trip, whose legitimate purpose is his "amateur" scientific research,
Ash describes his marine specimens confined in yellow pudding
bowls and later to his "regimen of dissection and magnification"
(p. 262). This research, though carried out for its own sake, relates
to the debate between the emerging evolutionary theory (Darwin-
ism) and Christian doctrine, and informs his poetry in terms of
theme and imagery. *Swammerdam* is the poetic monologue of a
seventeenth-century dutch microscopist who muses on the relation
between nature and God. Ash writes to Ellen: "I divagate without
discipline—my mind runs all over" (p. 256), but Ash is an "amateur" in the best sense, and for him art and science are mutually
enriching rather than mutually exclusive. The twentieth-century
critics, on the other hand are confined to a narrow specialization
within a secondary discipline which inhibits their creative impulses
and leads them to misread the primary object of study. Those who
are unable to look outwards or to pay proper attention to the text
without the narrowing lens of literary theory are presented as singu-
larly incapable of perceiving things as they are.

THE PROBLEM OF KNOWLEDGE

The novel maintains, however, that even a sympathetic textual
scholar is unable to gain full access to the truth, that any interpretation of documentary evidence is provisional. This must have been
brought home to Byatt following the publication of the first edition

of *Wordsworth and Coleridge*, which followed the current thinking that Wordsworth was more emotionally involved with his sister than with his wife. Subsequently, letters between Mary and Wordsworth were discovered which suggested that their marriage was in fact quite passionate, a discovery referred to in Cropper's lecture on "The Art of a Biographer" (p. 385). On the same lines Byatt has stated in interview: "You know that those letters you wrote, the ones that really mattered to you, were almost certainly destroyed by the person who received them, just so that the biographer shouldn't get at them." This statement is reproduced almost verbatim in the novel by Maud, when she says to the Baileys: "You know, if you read the collected letters of any writer — if you read her biography — you will always get a sense that there's something missing, something biographers don't have access to, the real thing, the crucial thing" (p. 89). It seems that the contemporary biographers are on their way to discovering "the crucial thing," when Maud deciphers Christabel's "dolly" poem and finds the cache of letters. The culmination of this literary paper chase, when the vultures finally gather round Ash's grave, is the discovery of the last letter which reveals the survival of Ash and Christabel's child, and the fact of Maud's ancestry, but the whole truth eludes their grasp. They construct a tragic ending to the Victorian lovers' story from the information they have, in which Ash dies in ignorance of his daughter's survival. But there is something omitted, a gap in the contemporary biographers' knowledge, which is revealed to the reader in the Postscript. In fact there is some evidence of this meeting, the fine plait of blonde hair in Ash's watch, but this is mistaken for Christabel's by both Ellen and those she has baited. As with Ellen's memories of her honeymoon, this final scene drives home the point that while the truth of a real life will elude even the most committed sleuth-biographer, fiction can provide the reader with imaginative access to a different kind of truth.

In an interview following the publication of *The Biographer's Tale* Byatt discusses the relation between biography and fiction:

I see biography as rather the opposite of writing a novel. You might think that you know a lot more about somebody in a biography than you will ever know about somebody in fiction. But, of course, the opposite is true. And I think that what fascinates me about biography is the way human beings always escape their biographers.

The dominant intellectual tenor in the late twentieth century has been described in Jean-François Lyotard's seminal account as "a suspicion of metanarratives." Metanarratives are those discourses, such as philosophy, religion, history, or science, which have traditionally claimed access to an ultimate truth or set of facts. Postmodern fiction, by presenting history as a written narrative, a *story* rather than a neutral collection of facts, participates in this condition. In *On Histories and Stories*, which is in part a defense of the kind of fiction that she writes, Byatt notes the many forms of current historical fiction: "parodic and pastiche forms, forms which fake documents or incorporate real ones, mixtures of past and present, hauntings and ventriloquism, historical versions of genre fictions — Roman and mediaeval and Restoration detective stories and thrillers." *Possession* alludes to the many forms in which the past can be written, thus undermining the idea of a simple, straightforward truth. Byatt has elsewhere pointed out the Victorians were relatively sophisticated in their understanding of history as narrative: "It is often seen as a modern discovery that history is necessarily fictive; it was in fact a pervasive nineteenth-century perception," although the examples she gives are of French historians. Fiction, of course, has never claimed the same sort of status, although it has traditionally been regarded as purveying certain truths about human nature or relations. Byatt quotes Browning's *The Ring and the Book* to this effect: "Art may tell a truth/Obliquely." In terms of postmodern thinking, fiction has the *advantage* over biography in that it purveys an imaginative or literary truth, rather than a literal, factual truth, and can do so with a kind of immediacy that a conventional biography cannot achieve. The novel does this quite simply by giving us direct access to events in the lives of the Victorian lovers as they unfold.

PARALLEL PLOTS

In *Possession*, message is reinforced by method so that as well as conveying its meaning directly through intrusive narration, the novel reveals its truth through dramatization. Hawthorne says that his tale is Romantic in its "attempt to connect a bygone time with the very present." Byatt draws parallels through the particular way she plots the novel so that the reader *experiences* the "historical" past as fictional present. The progress of Roland and Maud's romance is driven by their literary quest, to the point where the contemporary characters begin to feel haunted, as if their actions are determined by past lives. Even early on in their research, when Maud is driving away from Seal Court, she experiences an uncanny sense that her attention is feeding the past's vitality and making her own life ghostly. Much later on Roland is haunted by the same sense:

Somewhere in the locked-away letters, Ash had referred to the plot or fate which seemed to hold or drive the dead lovers. Roland thought, partly with precise postmodernist pleasure, and partly with a real element of superstitious dread, that he and Maud were being driven by a plot or fate that seemed, at least possibly, to be not their plot or fate but that of those others. (p. 421)

Although Roland and Maud are following the trail of the Victorian lovers, even they cannot be fully aware of the degree to which their experiences correspond. The point where the plot lines converge and the lives of the protagonists mimic each other most closely is in the middle of the novel (Chapters 13, 14, and 15), where the past abuts and intrudes upon the present.

In Chapter 13, Maud and Roland go to Yorkshire in the hope that they can establish whether Christabel and Ash were also there. We are given certain information about Maud and Roland: "They paced well together, though they didn't notice that; both were energetic striders" (p. 251). This signals to the reader their compatibility, but nothing else at the time. On their first night they eat a huge meal of vegetable soup, plaice with shrimps and profiteroles, served by a large "Viking woman," which is described in some detail. In the next chapter, they attempt, ironically and in vain, to evade their prey, and do something unconnected with the Victorians. They go to a place of natural interest, Boggle Hole:

They walked down through flowering lanes. The high hedges were thick with dog-roses, mostly a clear pink, sometimes white, with yellow-gold centres dusty with yellow pollen. The roses were intricately and thickly entwined with rampant wild honeysuckle, trailing and weaving creamy flowers among the pink and gold. (p. 268)

We are given here the kind of specific, local detail associated with literary realism, which can create a scene in the mind's eye of the reader, but in the main part carries little extra symbolic weight.

Chapter 15 begins with true analepsis — narrative movement back in time, motivated not through memory, and narrated as present action. There is no preamble to put the scene into context, so at first the reader is not aware of the chronological shift. Byatt comments on the shift in narrative mode in this scene in *On Histories and Stories*:

Fowles has said that the nineteenth-century narrator was assuming the omniscience of a god. I think rather the opposite is the case—this kind of fictive narrator can creep closer to the feelings and the inner life of characters—as well as providing a Greek chorus—than any first-person mimicry. In *Possession* I used this kind of narrator deliberately three times in the historical narrative—always to tell what the historians and biographers of my fiction never discovered, always to heighten the reader's imaginative entry into the world of the text.

The parallels between the couples are reinforced through action and imagery, so that the reader can identify both similarities and differences. Ash and Christabel are also served a huge meal of soup, fish, meat and pudding by another Viking descendent. When they go out walking, however, they notice the compatible rhythm of their step: "They both walked very quickly. 'We walk well together,' he told her. 'Our paces suit.'" (p. 280) We learn that Ash and Christabel have also visited Boggle Hole: "They had come across summer meadows and down narrow lanes between tall hedges thick with dog-roses, intricately entwined with creamy honeysuckle." (p. 286) While this period is Ash and Christabel's "honeymoon," the battle-scarred twentieth-century protagonists demonstrate their customary caution, but in a scene of analogous significance, they discuss their previous entanglements and Maud then looses her hair from its bindings, an event which is loaded with sexual significance. Through analepsis, parallel scenes, and linking imagery, Byatt allows the reader imaginative access to the past and thus to share something of Roland and Maud's "haunting" experience.

VENTRILOQUISM

There is another kind of possession or haunting in the novel, which Byatt describes in *On Histories and Stories; Possession*, she says, is "about . . . ventriloquism, love for the dead, the presence of [the] literary text as the voices of persistent ghosts or spirits." In writing *Possession*, Byatt was on a mission to rehabilitate Victorian poetry and answer "the disparaging mockery . . . of Leavis and T. S. Eliot." The Victorian age is still considered in academia to have been a high point for the novel and a low point for poetry. The Victorian novel was a vehicle for the discussion of social change, while new methods of production and rising literacy rates meant that it could experiment with new forms and reach a wider readership. Victorian poetry also addresses contemporary issues, such as the debate occasioned by discoveries in science and the related crisis in religious faith, but it is often presented as the dying gasp of Romanticism (Byron, Keats, Shelley, Wordsworth, Coleridge), which fails to offer anything innovative in the way of form. Byatt sees this novel as a counter to the blinkered modern literary criticism which imposes too rigid a template on the literary text:

Ventriloquism became necessary because of what I felt was the increasing gulf between current literary criticism and the words of the literary texts it in some sense discusses. Modern criticism is powerful and imposes its own narratives and priorities on the writings it uses as raw material, source, or jumping-off point.

An author is always a kind of ventriloquist, speaking through character or narrator, but in this novel the multiplicity of voices and other texts highlights this fact.

By parodying the modern literary theorists with their narrow, sex-obsessed, and jargon-ridden discourse, Byatt makes quite a good case for the Victorian thinker. Her method of rehabilitating the Victorian poets is similar: imitation. In *Passions of the Mind*, Byatt writes: "Parody and pastiche are particularly literary ways of pointing to the fictiveness of fiction, gloomily or gleefully." Pastiche denotes a medley of styles or, more often in literature, a work composed in the style of a well-known author. *Possession* is pastiche in both senses — a medley of styles and texts composed in a distinctive style. Parody is a comic imitation of an author's characteristics, but can suggest a "feeble imitation, travesty." When Maud and Roland visit Christabel's London home, a restoration job has made the house look newer than it would have done in Christabel's time. Maud describes the house as a "simulacrum," a word which connotes artificiality and inauthenticity. Byatt's "Victorian" poetry, as well as the diaries, letters, and modern literary criticism, is in some senses a simulacrum: the fictional texts are written to resemble closely Victorian originals.

In *On Histories and Stories*, Byatt describes the research behind Christabel's *Melusine*: "Before writing the poem, I read the dead writers Christabel read, the French monk, Jean d'Arras, John Keats and John Milton, whose snakes and Lamias inform her writing. For the Victorians were not simply Victorian. They read their past and resuscitated it." Her comments indicate that she intends a kind of authenticity rather than negative parody: "Writing Victorian words in Victorian contexts, in a Victorian order, and in Victorian relations of one word to the next was the only way I could think of to show one could hear the Victorian dead." By serving as a medium for the Victorian voice, she can make it "live" for the reader in a fictional context in the way that a critical commentary could not, just as she can present the life of a poet to the reader in a way which would be presumptuous in a conventional biography.

The poets, as well as their poems, are loosely based on Victorian originals. Ash is modeled most closely on Robert Browning, the poet who eloped with Elizabeth Barrett, and is best known for his dramatic monologues; instead of writing in a neutral poetic voice his poetic speakers tended to have a distinct fictional identity. Browning's customary subject matter was typically Victorian: faith and doubt, good and evil, the function of the artist. Compared to typical Victorians like Tennyson (except in *Maud*), Browning's style was relatively discordant and colloquial. There is also something of Tennyson in Ash, as Tennyson's studies of geological, astronomical and biological literature fed into his poetic treatment of contemporary topics.

Christabel is modeled on Emily Dickinson and Christina Rossetti, both "spinster" poets who lived secluded lives and fell in love with married men. Dickinson's poems, short lyrics which were often untitled, were in the main published posthumously. The characteristics of Dickinson's poetry were a flouting of conventional rhyme and meter, and an unconventional use of syntax and punctuation, especially a characteristic dash. Rossetti is associated with the Pre-Raphaelite poets, who favored mystical symbols and subjects from medieval myth. Her style is also somewhat unconventional, characterized by short, irregularly rhymed lines, but what is most striking about the poetry, including her *Poems for Children*, is its sinister and morbid qualities, together with a striking sensuality. Christabel, as she is described in the faded photograph examined by Roland and Maud, also has something of the look favored by the Pre-Raphaelites. Too much, however, should not be made of these correspondences; Byatt chooses to create fictional characters with a life independent of any historical model in order that they should have their own life.

The poems themselves serve various functions in the novel. In terms of the action, they act as ciphers for Maud and Roland, clues both to the state of mind and to events in the lives of their subjects. In some cases, as in Christabel's "dolly" poem, they provide tangible clues in the mystery quest, or evidence as in the shared imagery used in *Ask to Embla* and *Melusine*, which suggests to Maud and Roland that the pair were together in Yorkshire. But we also see misinterpretation of the poems; the untitled poem about Spilt Milk at the end of Chapter 19, is read by Maud as evidence that Christabel's child died, but this proves to be too literal an interpretation of the literary text.

The way the poems are positioned affects the way that they are read; in some cases the poetic text is read by one of the characters as part of the present action. Otherwise the poems, often extracts, occupy a more conventional place at the head of a chapter. The way that such epigraphs usually function is to point to or comment obliquely, or ironically on the subsequent action. The epigraph to Chapter 1 is from Ash's *The Garden of Proserpina* and refers to the ancient Greek equivalent of the Garden of Eden, containing the dragon-guarded golden fruit of the tree of life. As the myth goes, this fruit is stolen by Heracles and the poem thus has obvious reference to Roland's theft of the letter. What is most interesting is the description of Heracles as "the tricksy hero". He is an archetypal hero, famed for his strength, endurance, good humor, and appetite for food and women. The relation between this figure and the character we are subsequently introduced to is not immediately clear; there is an apparent disjunction between the lusty dragon-slayer and the small, self-effacing and not particularly handsome Roland. The narrator even tells us at one point that "he hardly qualified as a full-blooded departmental male" (p. 118). The connection between Heracles' and Roland's "tricksy" behavior here is perhaps designed to reassure the reader that Roland does indeed fit the heroic mold.

There is a short and gloomy poem of Christabel's at the heading of Chapter 7 which functions in a similar way. It contrasts the public arena of men's glorious martyrdom with the private decay of women's lives. As well as reflecting Christabel's preoccupations and personal circumstances, this is an obviously suitable epigraphic comment on Beatrice's professional life; as a young woman she fell in love with Ash's passionate voice in *Ask to Embla*, but was made to confine herself to Ellen's laundry lists and is now incarcerated in "a small cavern constructed of filing cabinets . . . almost bricked in by the boxes containing the diary and correspondence of Ellen Ash" (p. 27).

As well as providing Roland and Maud with clues to the narrative of Christabel and Ash's love affair, the poems reinforce for the reader the attraction between Roland and Maud and their connection between the Victorian lovers. Melusine is a creature of water, a mermaid who has seduced a mortal man and having married him, warned him never to watch her in the bath. Curiosity, of course, gets the better of him and he spies on her with disastrous consequences. Following Ellen's account of the poem in her journal in Chapter 7, in Chapter 8 Roland, out of a characteristic diffidence, waits for Maud to emerge from the bathroom at Seal Court. He eventually seeks to establish its vacancy by looking through the keyhole at which point, to his horror, Maud emerges, her hair "running all over her shoulders" and her silk robe appearing in the "half-light to be running with water, all the runnels of silk twisted about her body" (p. 147), making Maud a Melusine (except for the fact that instead of a silvery tail, she has a flannel nightie). Maud almost falls over his kneeling figure and both feel Ash's "kick galvanic"—the electrical manifestation of profound mutual attraction. The tragic end of *Melusine* does not prefigure a similar conclusion to Maud and Roland's incipient affair, but the correspondences between Victorian poem and contemporary action further reinforces the connection between the two couples.

FOLK/FAIRY TALES

Some of the inset fairy tales provide simpler allegories for the reader to decode. One of these, Christabel's "The Glass Coffin," again links the Victorian and modern couple and provides the reader with a neat predictive parallel of Maud and Roland's romance. "The Glass Coffin" is a rewriting of a Grimm fairy tale, in which a beautiful fair-haired princess is rescued from the glass coffin where she has been imprisoned by an evil wizard. The parallels are thrust under the nose of the reader fairly early on via Roland's internal monologue: "Blanche Glover called Christabel the Princess. Maud Bailey was a thin-skinned Princess. He was an intruder into their female fastnesses. Like Randolph Henry Ash" (p. 58). We read on with Roland to establish further connections for ourselves: the protagonist is not a prince, but a humble "little tailor, a good and unremarkable man" in search of work. Through a combination of good manners, resourcefulness, and courage, he proceeds eventually to open the glass coffin and waken the princess with a kiss. The little tailor knows the score, but departs from heroic type by suggesting to the Princess that she is free to remain unmarried if she wishes. The narrator glosses this for the reader: "And you may ask yourselves, my dear and most innocent readers, whether he spoke there with more gentleness or cunning, since the lady set such store on giving herself of her own free will" (p. 66). Of course, this story being a fairy-tale, "they did live happily ever after."

As with the parallel plot lines which are linked by repeated images, the inset poems and tales in the main narrative are effectively connected with the main narrative by a densely knitted tissue of imagery and allusion, explicitly linked by narrator or character, or apparently incidental, leaving the reader to draw his or her own conclusions. The physical and psychological similarities between the Princess in the tale, its author, and Maud have already been noted by Roland. The reader is already equipped to make further connections. Maud's physical description and haughty behavior cast her undeniably in the fairy tale princess mold. She is possessed of long, fair hair, a fair skin and a haughty manner and although she lives in a flat, she works in a tower. Unlike *Melusine*, this fairy-tale provides direction to Roland (as well as the reader), if he chooses to take it, on how to win Maud. It places him more firmly in the role of hero by providing a closer literary role model in the little tailor. The analogies already present in the tale suggest that Roland, if he continues to exercise resourcefulness and tact, is assured of his happy ending. The tale may also predict the conclusion of Christabel and Ash's relationship. Ash from the first proves a more importunate suitor than Roland, and though he conquers his princess, tempting her from her "female fastness," ultimately he loses her as the predatory Fergus lost Maud. The tale continues to echo in Maud's mind; later she thinks of Roland before sleep in unacknowledged terms of the little tailor: "He was a gentle and unthreatening being" (p. 141). And later still Byatt's narrator echoes Christabel's narrator in the lines: "But Maud would not again willingly have gone anywhere with Fergus. And she had more than willingly set out with Roland" (p. 421).

Other inset tales such as "The Threshold" and "Gode's Story" are less clearly relevant, but still have links with the main narratives. The "Childe" in the first of these stories, who is identified with Roland through literary allusion, is attracted by mystery. "Gode's Story," a dark Breton folk tale, speaks to Christabel's predicament and causes her discomfort though she is pretending to conceal her condition from those around her. In this story, a haughty girl who has spurned a freely-given gift from a suitor, is cursed for her pride. Though not explicit, there is the suggestion or suspicion that she has given birth to a child (and possibly killed it) because there is "blood on the straw." The miller's daughter denies both her attraction to the sailor and anything to do with the blood on the straw and is fated to die, pursued by a little imp — the child's spirit. The suitor, who subsequently marries, is condemned to the same fate. Christabel is, for her pride and denial, condemned to the loss of her lover, the loss of her daughter, and a metaphorical death of the spirit.

Connections proliferate through the various narrative strands of the novel. One significant example is the green, white and gold imagery associated with Christabel, the Princess in the glass coffin, Melusine, and Maud. Maud is first seen through Roland's eyes at the railway station: "He could not see her hair, which was wound tightly into a turban of peacock-feathered painted silk, low on her brow. Her brows and lashes were blond; he observed so much. She had a clean, milky skin, unpainted lips, clearcut features, largely composed" (pp. 38–39). The princess in her coffin has "a still white face, with long gold lashes on pale cheeks, and a perfect pale mouth. Her gold hair lay round her like a mantle" (p. 63). Christabel, when physically described on the train by the narrator, is dressed in grey, blue, green, and white. "She was very fair, pale skinned'; 'the bones were well-cut and the mouth an elegant curve" (p. 274). Later Ash observes her, as Roland has observed Maud: "lashes . . . silver, but thick enough to be visibly present. The face not kind. There was no kindness in the face. It was cut clean but not fine — strong-boned rather." Melusine is a milky luminous, white and green clad fairy:

> She wore a shift of whitest silk, that stirred
> With her song's breathing, and a girdle green
> As emerald or wettest meadow-grass.
>
> Her living hair was brighter than chill gold . . .

> It was a face
> Queenly and calm, a carved face and strong
> Nor curious, nor kindly, nor aloof,
> But self-contained and singing to itself. (pp.
> 296–97)

As well as these physical similarities Maud and Christabel share a psychological template to a degree, which is also allegorized in "The Glass Coffin." Where the princess in this story is literally imprisoned, Christabel is constrained by circumstance and convention, and Maud is metaphorically imprisoned, bent on self-preservation. The difference is that in fairy tales princesses are imprisoned against their will, Maud's reserve is more complicated, a learned defense, in simple terms she is once bitten twice shy after her affair with Fergus. Maud thinks despairingly of "her bright safe box" and in the narrative this is followed almost immediately by the letter from Christabel to Ash comparing herself to an egg, "doorless and windowless, whose life may slumber on till she be Waked" (p. 137), both egg and box are symbols analogous to the glass coffin. Of course the physical and possibly even the psychological similarities between Christabel and Maud are naturalized when it is revealed that the two are literally related, while the fairy Melusine is Christabel written in her own work. Arguably such connections throughout the text prepare the reader for this conclusion as well as linking the narrative strands.

The links between inset or epigraph texts and action can be subtle. For example, there is a poem by Christabel at the head of Chapter 8 which uses snow imagery. This functions to set the scene; Maud and Roland are going through the letters at a freezing Seal Court where it also begins to snow (the narrative description of this snow falling has lyrical echoes of Joyce's "The Dead"). But there is also a metaphorical cold; Maud has already been associated with whiteness (chastity, untouchability) and an emotional lack of warmth. She is — like Christabel — a "chilly mortal." Here, in the freezing library she assures Joan Bailey that she is warm enough, she creates a distinct frostiness in the atmosphere which is perceived by a disappointed Roland. This scene also demonstrates the way in which imagery and diction from fairy tales pervades the narrative. In the library, "There was a faint flash of colour in her ivory cheeks. As though the cold brought out her proper life, as though she were at home in it" (p. 129). This echoes Maud's earlier blush at her flat in Lincoln, the language used alludes to fairy tale: "Red blood stained the ivory" (p. 50). Red and white color imagery is prevalent in fairy tales such as Snow White. Trapped by the snow into staying the night, explicit reference is made to fairy stories as Roland is reminded by Maud's bed of the "Real Princess and the pea." Earlier in the novel, again in Maud's flat: "She made him up a bed on the high white divan in her living-room . . . a real bed with laundered sheets and pillows in emerald green cotton cases. And a white down quilt, tumbled out of a concealed drawer beneath" (p. 55). The slight archaisms: "laundered"; "a white down quilt" and hints of mystery: "a concealed drawer beneath" blur the boundaries between the two narrative forms. Roland is about to read 'The Glass Coffin', and before he goes to sleep thinks of "the Real Princess, suffering the muffled pea" (p. 58).

In fairy-tale stories (though perhaps not the darker folk-tales) the frozen ice princess would be warmed up by the prince, although in Byatt's fairy tale "Cold" an ice princess is liberated only by living in her proper element. Roland finally does take possession of Maud so that "all her white coolness that grew warm against him" (p. 507) — a conventional fairy-tale/romance ending. Indeed the final scene between Roland and Maud has touches of the fairy-tale as the consummation, which would of course be omitted from a real fairy-tale, takes place in a feather bed after they have blown out a candle. The reader may not consciously attend to all of these allusions, in fact the subtler echoes might work more effectively at a subliminal level, but by a variety of means: direct narrative comment, dialogue and internal monologue, image and literary allusion, the threads of narrative are interwoven in the text and in the mind of the reader.

While this provides a sense of artistic coherence, the confusion or coincidence of literary present and fairy-tale may stretch the reader's credulity. Byatt writes in the collection *Passions of the Mind* that "Traditional realism works with probabilities, correcting the melodramatic or fairy-tale expectations of romance," and in *Possession* the implications of the initial epigraphic quotations suggest that in this novel she eschews realism in favor of romance. The extract from Nathaniel Hawthorne's *The House of the Seven Gables*, asserts that the genre allows the writer "a certain latitude" as distinct from the novel which aims "at a very minute fidelity, not merely to the possible, but to the probable and ordinary course of man's experience." This gives the author leeway to construct improbable coincidences or fantastic occurrences, which would not fit with the stricter demands for verisimilitude, the unbroken illusion of reality, of the novel. But romance and realism are not mutually exclusive — there is no strict demarcation between the two; the novel itself is an elastic genre, as is the ability of the reader to assimilate the fantastic when entering into the fictional world. Events, and characters, do not have to be realistic in the sense of *probable*, but real in the sense that they are made to live in the reader's imagination.

MORALS AND ENDINGS

Byatt has been critical of John Fowles' "experimental alternative endings to [*The French Lieutenant's Woman*], which painfully destroy the narrative 'reality' of the central events." She suggests that the fictional world in this novel is too rudely revealed as a sham:

These alternative endings are neither future nor conditional, but fixed, Victorian, narrative past. They therefore cancel each other out, and cancel their participants, rendering Fowles as arbitrary a puppet-maker as he declared his desire not to be. For the writer, whilst the plural endings are possibilities in the head, they intensify the reality of the future world. For the reader, now, they reduce it to paperiness again.

A postmodern novelist has a problem with endings, as the narrator tells us (obliquely): "Coherence and closure are deep human desires that are presently unfashionable. But they are always both frightening and enchantingly desirable" (p. 422). Byatt also provides two endings, both of them happy in their way, without reducing the fictional world to "paperiness." She finds a compromise between coherence and closure and the postmodern game.

The beginning of the end of the novel is marked by Roland's discovery of his poetic voice in Chapter 26. This chapter is headed by a long extract from Ash's *The Garden of Proserpina*, which describes an edenic age of language when there was no disjunction between words and things: "They made names and poetry/ The things *were* what they named and made them" (p. 464). This is truly a mythic age for a poststructuralist, for whom the orthodox theory of language admits only an arbitrary relation between a word and the thing in the world it describes. There is also a disquisition over several pages on the nature of writing and reading, the power of words. Roland is a literary critic, who does not simply dissect, but admires. As we have seen, this secondary and sometimes subvervient position, can dampen any primary creative impulse and Roland is also potentially inhibited by the dead-end of structuralist thought: "He had been taught that language was essentially inadequate, that it could never speak what was there, that it only spoke itself" (p. 473). But Roland's reading of Ash proves to be inspirational: "What had happened to him was that the ways in which it

could be said had become more interesting than the idea that it
could not." The discovery of this poetic voice is crucial in respect
of the central theme, possession. Unlike Blackadder, whose creative
impulses have been long since stifled, Roland acquires, through
some mystical process, a poetic voice. This is not a secondary,
critical voice, not even derivative of Randolph Henry Ash: Roland
"began to think of words, words came from some well in him. . . .
He could hear, or feel, or even almost see, the patterns made by a
voice he didn't yet know, but which was his own" (p. 475). When
Roland finally goes public about his initial theft of Ash's letter to
the assembled party at Beatrice Nest's house, it is described by the
narrator as "the moment of dispossession, or perhaps the word was
exorcism" (p. 480), but he can let go because he now owns his
poetic voice.

The following chapter is headed by a poem by Ash on the
inevitable movement of life towards its ending, and the compulsion
to know — so the novel draws to its conclusion. In spite of the
sinister event the characters are about to get involved in, there is an
air of romantic comedy — in the Shakespearean sense — not only do
Roland and Maud get together, but the sullen Val has found an
apparently suitable mate in the suave Euan MacIntyre. This is
foregrounded by: " 'And all's well that ends well,' said Euan. 'This
feels like the ending of a Shakespearean comedy' " (pp. 482–83).
But it isn't quite the ending. The novel descends into gothic farce
with the grave robbing scene and thence to the climax of the
contemporary romance narrative.

When Roland and Maud finally go to bed with each other, the
language in which their lovemaking is described is significant:

And very slowly and with infinite gentle delays and delicate diversion and
variations of indirect assault Roland finally, to use an outdated phrase,

entered and took possession of all her white coolness that grew warm against him so that there seemed to be no boundaries . . . (507).

The words that Byatt has used: "diversions," "assault," have connotations of combat, the fact that there are no longer any boundaries, suggest "breaking," which would seem to be antipathetic to both characters. But the boundaries have fallen or been lowered because of Roland's gentleness, the postmodern knight has worthily won his fair lady. In spite of the use of the word "possession" to describe his love-making, Roland represents only minimal threat to Maud's autonomy. The union of Roland, who was Ash's literary "disciple" and Maud, who is Christabel's literal descendent, in some sense represents the eventual happy ending for the Victorian lovers themselves. Byatt thus contrives a fairy-tale ending to both the Victorian and the contemporary romance.

But even this is not the end. When faced with the box stolen from Ash's grave, Maud echoes his poem when she says: "We need the end of the story" (p. 498). But as Blackadder suggests, knowledge is incomplete and they construct from their incomplete understanding, a far more tragic conclusion than was the case, assuming from Christabel's final letter that Ash never knew of his daughter. The Postscript reveals a different ending to the story. So finally both Byatt and the reader have the best of both worlds: Byatt reminds the reader of the provisional nature of historical knowledge by creating imaginative access to a fictional truth.

3

The Novel's Reception

There was an almost universal enthusiasm for *Possession*, from the first review to the later articles which attempted to dissect the novel's success. The first function of a review is to describe and give a flavour of the novel to the reader. In the U.K. Byatt's work was fairly well known to a significant readership, but *Possession* represents an exaggeration of certain of Byatt's traits. Word limits and deadlines must be particularly irksome when reviewing a novel of this complexity, and most reviewers could only flag the major themes and obvious distinguishing features in the book: the parallel Victorian and contemporary love stories, the literary pastiche, and so on. Another function of early reviews is to "place" a novel in its literary context, in relation to previous works by the same author and to current literary trends. In the *Times* (1 March 1990), Nicola Murphy compares the novel to Umberto Eco's *The Name of the Rose* and Graham Swift's *Waterland* because of their scholar-detectives, though she misses the obvious parallel in the latter's treatment of historical and narrative time. In the *Times Literary Supplement* (2 March 1990), Richard Jenkyns marshals a gallery of American *and* British comparisons: David Lodge's *Nice Work* and

Changing Places; Angus Wilson's *Anglo-Saxon Attitudes*, Margaret Drabble's *The Ice Age*, Alison Lurie's *The Truth About Lorin Jones*.

The U.S. reviewers had a slightly more difficult task, in that Byatt's work was more likely to be unfamiliar to their readership, but many assume familiarity with both the English literary tradition and postmodern fiction in general. Two reviewers at the *New York Times*, Jay Parini and Christopher Lehmann-Haupt, relate the novel to its British and international literary context. Parini refers to the English tradition and South American postmodernism, like Jenkyns comparing *Possession* to the campus comedy of David Lodge and suggesting that Sir George Bailey is a character from the comic novels of P. G. Wodehouse. He also describes the secret of Ash's grave as "Dickensian." Lest the American reader be expecting an untaxing romp, he goes on: "As *Possession* progresses, it seems less and less like the usual satire about academia and more like something by Jorge Luis Borges". Lehmann-Haupt identifies Byatt with Anglo-American postmodernism, identifying as its "precursors" John Fowles' *The French Lieutenant's Woman* and Charles Palliser's *The Quincunx*.

The primary function of the review is to evaluate the work, to recommend to the reader. Prior to the publication of *Possession*, Byatt had been well respected by the literary establishment and her novels had received favorable reviews. Reviewers were given to praising the "intelligence" of the work, noting her novels' ambition, as well as her powers of description and literary language. Early British reviews of *Possession* were favorable, but did tend to qualify their enthusiasm with reservations. The first review in the *Times*, recommends the novel in so far as it is the Novel of the Week column, but is largely descriptive. Jenkyns in the second corrects Byatt on a few anachronisms but concedes that "pedantry must quickly give way to admiration for a brilliant achievement of sheer technique" and refers to the novel as a *tour de force*. He spends some time critiquing character, asserting that "the impersonation of Christabel is a triumph," and going on to convince the reader that she's a fully rounded character: "We are able to walk round Christabel and see her from different angles." Jenkyns, in this substantial review, is able to point to the way that a fictional life allows an imaginative understanding that a historical portrait might not. Ash, he finds less convincing, arguing that he is *too* typical a Victorian — a cipher rather than a living being. The twentieth-century characters, furthermore, "can be cardboard. . . . Roland remains shadowy, and Maud never comes alive." Jenkyns is furthermore critical of the novel's metafictional passages, positively damning "one or two passages of would-be post-modern self-reflexiveness, which merely take us back to the university novel at its most arch and banal" — a mistake in a novel whose virtue is its "solidity." He concludes, slightly stiffly, that the novel is "a fine work" and likely to be "one of the most memorable novels of the 1990s." A review in the *Evening Standard*, describing the novel's treatment of themes as "delicious" and "profound," declares that Byatt "is ripening into our best novelist," suggesting perhaps that *Possession* may not be quite the pinnacle of her achievement. *Cosmopolitan* magazine nailed its colors to the mast, calling the novel "a triumphant success on every level." Many of the reviews, like Jenkyns, predicted the particular success of the novel: the *Cosmopolitan* review stated that "*Possession* will be the sensation of the year," while the review in the *Spectator* praised, but hedged its bets: "A brilliant start to the publishing season, and one which it will be very difficult to overtake."

British broadsheet reviewers had criticised as well as complimented the erudition prominently displayed in Byatt's previous novels. Writing in the *Sunday Times* (4 March 1990), Peter Kemp asserts that "literary allusions can be strewn around Byatt's narratives with daunting voluminousness" and refers snidely to "bookish baggage" and "a slurry of cross-reference." He finally judges that *Posses-*

sion has avoided the pitfall of intellectualism and asserts that Byatt's "clever, discursive talent at last finds it form." The tone of this review is enthusiastic overall and its own rhetoric rather extravagant, presumably designed to convey the energy and plenitude of the novel: "this cerebral extravaganza of a story zig-zags with unembarrassed zest across an imaginative terrain bristling with symbolism and symmetries, shimmering with myth and legend." Kemp particularly praises Byatt's "uncanny flair" in "the brilliant sequence of pastiche poems" and also remarks on Byatt's achievement in *realizing* both contemporary and Victorian worlds. His one criticism is "the occasional tendency of its contemporary scenes to come too close to the tones and techniques of Iris Murdoch's novels."

There were a few reports of *Possession*'s win of the *Irish Times* prize and Booker nomination in the States, but the novel was not substantially reviewed there until its publication after the Booker. U.S. reviewers were thus already aware of the novel's critical and commercial success in Britain, and whether or not this informed the tenor of their reviews, it is notable there was, relatively speaking, less carping and much more unadulterated enthusiasm. The *Washington Post* (October 17 1990), contained a review by Michael Dirda, which positively smothers the book in praise:

Book critics are paid to offer informed, careful judgements, full of erudition or good sense or both, but sometimes all we really want to say about a novel is "Wow!" A. S. Byatt's *Possession* is that kind of book. You turn its last page feeling stunned and elated, happy to have had the chance to read it. At once highly traditional and eminently postmodern, this is a novel for every taste[.]

Other reviews, also overwhelmingly positive, followed. The phrase *tour de force* was used by at least three different reviewers. Parini closes with a ringing endorsement of "this georgeously written novel"; "*Possession* is a tour de force that opens every narrative device of English fiction to inspection without, for a moment, ceasing to delight."

Lehmann-Haupt is equally complimentary at times, opening with "wonderfully extravagant", describing the novel as "a witty and sometimes even moving commentary on the cycles of history and the contrast between the pre-Darwinian age and the age of post-modernism." Lehmann-Haupt, however, has reservations about the substantial pastiche element of the novel, stating that "her brilliant mimicry of Victorian poetry too often reflects its tedium as well as its complexly patterned obsessiveness." More idiosyncratically, he "bridles at the liberty she takes in describing at first hand certain scenes involving Ash and LaMotte that no one could plausibly have witnessed"; it isn't clear why Lehmann-Haupt objects to Byatt's omniscient narrator at this point, he goes on to argue that "After all, Nathaniel Hawthrone"s definition of a romance, which serves as her novel's epigraph, although granting "a certain latitude", still insists on a rigid subjection to the laws of art." He closes, however, by asserting that Byatt's effort of imagination has "to a remarkable degree succeeded."

The novel was thus ringingly endorsed by the U.S. critics and further promoted for the Christmas market in various "best of 1990" fiction lists, including the *New York Times* Editors' Choice: The Best Books of 1990 (Sunday 2 December) — significant, presumably for the Christmas market. It was also listed in the Sunday *Washington Post* Recommended List (2 December): "Best novels of 1990? Start with A. S. Byatt's *Possession*."

Early reviews, which effectively preview the novel for the reader, to some degree institute trends since they act as recommendations to the reader. These may be followed by more general review articles, if the success of the novel warrants it. Mervyn Rothstein's

New York Times article, 'Best Seller Breaks Rule On Crossing The Atlantic' (31 January 1991), examines the unprecedented success of a Booker winner in America. As well as discussing the novel's marketing and publicity, Rothstein is complimentary about the literary pastiche, saying that

The most dazzling aspect of *Possession* is Ms. Byatt's canny invention of letters, poems and diaries from the 19th century. She quotes whole vast poems by Ash and LaMotte, several of which struck me, anyway, as highly plausible versions of Browning and Rossetti and are beautiful poems on their own.

In a rather populist interview article in the *New York Times*, 26 May 1991 (Sunday), which eschews literary analysis, Mira Stout describes the book as 'a winning combination of snob appeal and genuine accessibility, presenting a familiar 'Masterpiece Theater' Britain of dusty libraries, fumbling academics and fiendish baronets, souped up with highbrow postmodernist conceits and middlebrow reader-friendliness'. Referring to the interview, but presumably paraphrasing Byatt, Stout cites Byatt's admission that the book succeeded because of a 'crowd-pleasing technique' and explains "Characters have more zing." This interview presents Byatt herself to the American reading public, whose interest had presumably been piqued by the success of the novel, in an unintentionally comic manner:

Clad in a mannish black fedora and starchy loden overcoat, Byatt looks a picture of assured authority, a cross between a school headmistress and the Foreign Secretary. Yet close up, she is soft, dimpled and plump, with a strikingly feminine cupid's-bow mouth and dishevelled grey-brown curls. Beneath her animated, bulldog-firm manner, she often displays surprising vulnerability.

Not only does this description smack of a rather lowly form of fiction, there is an intrinsic irony in this kind of article, given Byatt's comments on and strictures against biography, but they sustain interest in and further endorse the novel. The truism that success breeds success has some relevance in this context, in that journalism, even literary journalism, has a herd-following tendency. Without any substantial interest to sustain it, however, a topic will be dropped, suggesting that in the end public opinion presides. *Possession*'s reception by the reading public is indicated most clearly by its sales performance, which is discussed in the next section of the guide.

4

The Novel's Performance

Possession is the novel that made Byatt an international name, reinforcing her reputation in Britain and ensuring the commercial success of both future novels and her backlist. It has been a phenomenally successful book, managing that rather difficult feat of winning critical acclaim, prestigious literary prizes, and the popular appeal of the best seller. Not only did *Possession* win the Booker Prize in October 1990, it also won the *Irish Times*/Aer Lingus Award (before the Booker) and was subsequently short-listed for the Whitbread Award (Best Novel category). After the Booker win, *Possession* made the difficult transatlantic crossing to America, where it was received with critical admiration and and took up residence on the best seller lists, classifying both as a "fast seller," and manifesting staying power. It has been translated into more than fifteen languages and has now been made into a film.

In Britain the novel was published in hardback by Chatto & Windus in the Spring of 1990, with an initial print run of 29,000.[1] It was reported in *The Times* on 18 October, that the Booker Prize, which is well publicized in Britain, particularly in bookshops where the contenders are often positioned in special displays, had led to a sell out of this initial print run. Richard Todd casts doubt on this figure, suggesting that it may represent a journalistic inflation of the facts, but hardback sales account for only a fraction of most fiction sales because hardbacks are so expensive. The paperback was published by Vintage in February 1991, at a considerably higher price than the average paperback, but this would not necessarily have put off casual browsers since there was a lot of book for the money. By this time not only would pre- and post-Booker publicity and favorable reviews have entered the book-buying public's consciousness, but word of mouth would have spread. It was classified as a "fast seller" in a table of 1991 paperbacks and came 26th overall with total sales reaching 250,000 copies.

Initially Byatt could not find an American publisher and the novel was not published in the U.S. until after the Booker Prize win in October of 1990. Whereas Byatt had enough of a reputation in Britain to ensure some sales, further consolidated by good initial reviews and the Booker nomination, in America her reputation did not precede her to the same extent. The U.S. publishers, Random House, were clearly nervous about the novel's reception and proposed some changes. The first of these was to cut substantially the poem elements of the novel. The second was to make Roland a more obviously heroic, perhaps Herculean, character, or, as a *Wall Street Journal* article puts it: "Ms Byatt . . . says her editors at Random House insisted she make her main character . . . a sexier guy." Some concession was made and American readers got a few extra sentences designed to convince them of his romantic-heroic qualifications. He is given "a smile of amused friendliness" that often "aroused feelings of warmth, and sometimes more, in many women," lines which in their banality appear to parody the Harlequin romance genre. In the main argument Byatt won out, with apparently no detrimental effect on subsequent sales. It appeared that Random House was playing it safe with a relatively small hardback print run of 9,000, but aggressive marketing and rave reviews sent the novel into best seller lists where it stayed for approximately six months. The hardback sold between 90,000 and 100,000 copies and at times up to 10,000 copies per week. *Possession* also did well in other English-speaking countries such as Australia and Canada, and in translation in mainland Europe (particularly in Germany). Part of the appeal for other European readers, may have been the novel's allusion to European folk and fairy tales, aided by a significant academic interest in these forms. Also, because the tradition of experimental postmodernist metafiction is also better established in countries like France and Italy, where philosophy is taught in schools and metaphysics is not regarded with fear and loathing, than in Britain where intellectual predilections tend towards empiricism and realism.

Early in 1991, journalists began to mull over the novel's appeal and commercial success, perhaps helping to sustain its market position. Although early reviews mentioned the Prize, and often the *Irish Times*/Aer Lingus prize as well, *The Wall Street Journal* reported (6 December 1990) that at that point the Booker boost had upped British sales of the hardback to 60,000, which the author judged a figure "stunning for anyone other than a Jeffrey Archer or a Jilly Cooper. Still of significance for early U.S. sales is Mervyn Rothstein's article, "Best Seller Breaks Rule On Crossing The Atlantic" (31 January 1991). The "rule" of the title is a negative one in that, as Rothstein asserts, Booker Prize success does not guarantee success in the United States, but at the time of writing the article the novel had been on the *New York Times* best seller list for six weeks and had also received critical acclaim. John Sterling, editor in chief of U.S. publisher of Houghton Mifflin, is reported by Rothstein as saying in that the influence of the Booker Prize in the United States had begun to rise with Kazuo Ishiguro's *The Remains of the Day* (the 1989 winner).

Richard Todd's book on the Booker, *Consuming Fictions*, contains a substantial essay which examines the success of *Possession*. Aside from its intrinsic literary merits, external factors which may have contributed to the novel's success in the United States were the early, highly laudatory early reviews. Susan Kamil, executive editor of Random House, is quoted in Todd as connecting good reviews with sales: "It wasn't just that the book was well reviewed, it was celebrated. And the celebration of the book, the tone of the reviews, pulled the buyers onto the bookstores." Rothstein cites various factors which might have accounted for the novel's success, including the increasingly influential Booker Prize, the celebratory reviews, aggressive advertising, and the cover design of the American edition.

The U.S. design, whose central image, *The Beguiling of Merlin* by British Pre-Raphaelite painter Edward Burne-Jones, shows a somewhat mournful seductress winsomely toying with her floating garments and standing over a rather droopy-looking Merlin (modeled on Dante), against a floral and bosky backdrop. This image, chosen by Byatt, alludes to the story of Merlin's seduction by Vivien, and suggests a host of literary texts in addition to the Arthurian legend. The supernatural seductress was a figure of particular fascination to many nineteenth-century poets including Keats, Tennyson, and Sir Walter Scott, and appears in Christabel's *Melusine* and "The Threshold." Burne-Jones' image is reversed on the back cover, echoing in visual form the parallel narratives. The success of a book cover, however, is not based on literary reference but on a more immediate visual appeal, and this one is intriguing and striking. The British cover is less inventive; it comprises a collage of images including flowers, hair, lines of text and, as its focus, the Pre-Raphaelite head of a woman, slightly blurred, the whole an umber color as if sepia-tinted, and distinctly feminine. The collage effect is appropriate to *Possession*, but the design is typical of its time, one of many, and would simply have signaled to the bookshop browser that between the covers lay literary fiction.

Though both reviewers and ordinary readers in America embraced *Possession*, there was a certain generosity in so doing, considering the way that Byatt treats her American characters: Cropper, who is a cipher for greed and a certain kind of vulgarity; and Leonora, who is large, loud, and crude. This is not to say that all the English characters are sympathetic, but the Americans represent national caricatures. Jay Parini, who regards both American and English academics as caricatures, describes Mortimer Cropper as "a cross between Leon Edel and Liberace." Otherwise the "Englishness" of the novel, which obtrudes most obviously in the novel's diction, as well as settings such as the British Museum, down-at-heel glamour of Seal Court, or the quaint eighteenth-century inn of the final scene have obvious "tourist" appeal. Characteristics such as the shabbiness and hopelessness of Blackadder and Beatrice, the sullenness of Val, the poshness of Maud, could equally well have confirmed the stereotypical expectations of American readers.

Byatt has always been of interest to the academy, but quite often tended to be discussed along with other post-war "women writers." With the publication of *Possession* scholarly attention has shifted and increased. Partly because, in spite of Byatt's objections, the novel fits very well into the postmodern category and because of its erudition and incorporation (as well as derision) of postmodern theory, it has a particular appeal in the literary academy. It is studied most often on undergraduate contemporary/postmodern literature courses, and is also the subject of numerous postgraduate theses. This academic market, as Byatt concedes, can keep a book in print.

As well as winning the £20,000 Booker Prize, the indirect financial gains for Byatt and her publishers were considerable. The success of *Possession* created a marketing opportunity not merely for the novel itself, but for the whole backlist (as well as making the commercial success of Byatt's future output more likely). As Todd explains, after the Booker, Vintage, the paperback imprint of Random House who also owned Byatt's hardback publisher Chatto & Windus, reissued most of Byatt's backlist. Todd also points out that the "post-*Possession* sales of the earlier fiction titles have in every case exceeded ten times the original hardback sales." Although there seems little doubt that *Possession* materially affected the sales of the backlist, it is worth noting that prior to the Booker win, Penguin editions of the novels had also gone into reprint.

Although Byatt has said that she was confident of the novel's success, stating in interview: "I knew people would like it. It's the only one I've written to be liked, and I did it partly to show off," no one can predict a best seller, certainly not U.S. publishers, given their initial disinterest in the novel. Whatever the reasons for the novel's spectacular success, it had a great impact on journalists, critics and the reading public, not to mention Byatt herself. Even in 1991 she is reported to have been tired of talking about *Possession* and frustrated by demands made on her time by journalists that the success of the novel occasioned.

THE FILM

Byatt's work has already been turned into film; "Morpho Eugenia," one of the novellas in *Angels and Insects*, starring Patsy Kensit and directed by Philip Haas, was launched at the Cannes Film Festival in 1995. Todd remarks that "The paperback tie-in of *Angels and Insects* in turn aroused fresh interest in the filming of *Possession*." This interest was sustained, and at the time of writing this Guide, the film is just about to be released, starring Gwyneth Paltrow as Maud, Aaron Eckhart as Roland with Jeremy Northam and Jennifer Ehle as Ash and Christabel. The film, directed by Neil LaBute and produced by USA Films and Warner Brothers, was rather a long time in the making and the release date has already been delayed several times. The presence of Gwyneth Paltrow and the backing of Warner Brothers suggests that this is not an "art house" film, but a mainstream movie, and according to Greg Schmitz at upcoming-movies.com, "is thought to be one of USA Films' Oscar big guns." The question, therefore, of how the more literary elements of the novel are dealt with in film is interesting. Clues may lie in other films of postmodern literary texts. There has been a precedent set in *The French Lieutenant's Woman*, in which the parallel narratives are emphasized by the fact that the same actors play both Victorian and contemporary roles. Certain elements of *Possession* would seem to lend themselves to film, in particular the Postscript. The inset texts and authorial intrusion and literary allusion are less easily adapted to film, though precedent has again been set with the film version of Angela Carter's story "The Company of Wolves." In Carter's text, the main story—a postmodern version of *Little Red Riding Hood*, is preceded by short summaries of more traditional wolf folk tales, and one of these is inset into the main action of the film. The technical problem with *Possession* is the incidence and variety of these inset texts. In short the complexity of the novel presents a great number of technical problems. As reported by Philip French in *The Guardian*, Byatt declared herself happy with the movie so far after visiting the set: "You never know, of course, how things will turn out, but the auguries are good."

5

Further Reading and Discussion Questions

Discussion Questions

1. At the end of the novel the reader is presented with the meeting between Ash and his daughter which the twentieth-century characters do not know took place. Where else does Byatt withhold information in the novel? Is the reader ever made aware of information to which s/he is not allowed access? What point is Byatt making by withholding significant information from characters and/or reader?

2. Byatt's American publishers were worried that Roland's character would not be sufficiently heroic or attractive for the American readership, and asked Byatt to insert a few lines, making it clear to the reader that Roland is actually quite attractive to women (see Section 4). Was this necessary? What techniques are used to convince the reader that Roland should employ the hero's role and do they work?

3. Mortimer Cropper is an unsympathetic character and a poor biographer. Can we simply divide the characters into "good" and "bad" biographers, or is the distinction unclear? What are the

moral implications of Roland and Maud's deception of Val and Leonora when they escape to Yorkshire and Brittany and when they refuse to intervene and prevent the violation of Ash's grave? What is the moral status of the "hungry reader," who wants to know the end of the story?

4. There are obvious parallels drawn between Christabel and Maud. How do the obstacles faced by the Victorian poet and the twentieth-century critic compare and what political point might Byatt be making about the status of women in the two historical periods?

5. The American publishers originally wanted Byatt to cut substantial quantities of the invented Victorian poetry, though in the end the text remained uncut. Byatt has also said in interview that she wrote the novel with the reader's attention span in mind. Did you "skip" parts of the novel and, if so, which parts? Did you feel obliged to read the poetry, but feel frustrated that it halted the narrative action? If you read the poetry did you enjoy it *as* poetry or read it for the light it threw on the rest of the narrative?

6. Look again at Ash and Christabel's conversation at the end of Chapter 15. Is the connection between the quotations and the narrative context made clear? By including such allusions does the novel assume the reader's acquaintance with the texts themselves and is such familiarity necessary? One critic, Alex Clark, wrote of *The Matisse Stories*: "the emotional impact that Byatt has the power to make is lessened by an oppressive sense that the author is superior to the reader." Could the reader of *Possession* be made to feel inferior to its author?

7. Read some of the Victorian poems suggested below and compare them to the "fictional" poems in *Possession*. How closely do Byatt's compositions mirror the Victorian originals? Do you think

there are elements of parody in Byatt's poems, or do they simply
convey the author's admiration for the Victorians?

8. Compare the treatment of the poems with a "real" feminist essay
by Hélène Cixous (see below) and Leonora's analysis of *Melusine*
in Chapter 13. Are there significant differences? What is the
author's implicit attitude towards Leonora's brand of literary criticism?

9. *Possession* has often been compared with John Fowles' *The
French Lieutenant's Woman* (brief details below). Byatt, however,
has expressed reservations about the technical success of the
latter novel, particularly the way that the novel's construction
militates against the reality of the fictional world. Does the past
action seem more vivid than the present in *Possession*, or are
both Victorian and contemporary characters given equal weight?
Compare the degree to which the fictional world is made real in
the two novels

Suggested Further Reading

Novels by Byatt

The specific editions referred to in this Guide are cited after the
first publication date.

Possession. London: Vintage, 1991.
Shadow of a Sun (1964); second edition published as *The Shadow of the
Sun: A Novel*. London: Vintage, 1991.
The Game (1967). London: Penguin, 1983.
The Virgin in the Garden (1978). London: Penguin, 1981.
Still Life (1985). London: Penguin, 1986.
Babel Tower (1996). London: Vintage, 1987.
The Biographer's Tale. London: Chatto & Windus, 2000.

Collected Short Stories

Sugar and Other Stories (1987). Byatt's first collection of stories is unified by the themes of isolation, death, and grief and is highly autobiographical.

Angels and Insects (1992). This comprises two novellas. The first, "Morpho Eugenia," which is set in 1859, demonstrates Byatt's preoccupation with Victorian natural sciences (entymology). The second, "The Conjugial Angel," explores the Victorian fascination with the supernatural and contains a spiritualist who is both genuine and fake. It also contains a "real" historical figure in the person of Emily Jesse, Alfred Tennyson's sister.

The Matisse Stories (1993). A reviewer of *Sugar* states that her prose "seems to paint rather than to describe." *Still Life* uses the vivid color imagery of the post-impressionists, particularly Van Gogh, and these stories are inspired by another post-impressionist Henri Matisse. The three stories have middle-aged protagonists suffering different forms of female malaise, but each ends on a note of qualified optimism.

The Djinn in the Nightingale's Eye: Five Fairy Stories (1994). A "feminist" collection, which contains two of the fairy-tales from *Possession*: "The Glass Coffin" and "Gode's Story." "The Story of the Eldest Princess" is, as Byatt has explained, an allegory of her own life. The title story is based on the archetypal structure of fairy-tale but has a contemporary setting.

Elementals: Stories of Fire and Ice (1998). A collection of stories again about isolation. The princess protagonist in "Cold" has echoes of the frosty Maud.

Selected and Collected Non-Fiction by Byatt

Degrees of Freedom: The Novels of Iris Murdoch (1965). This was republished by Vintage in 1994, changing the subtitle to "The Early Novels of Iris Murdoch" and adding a Foreword and further essays. Byatt traces the connections between Murdoch's moral philosophy, literary theory, and fiction. She writes in the Foreword of her dismay at the "insistence on making severe judgments of tone and texture, a function of . . . the serious criticism of the time," which fails to convey her true enthusiasm for the novels. She blames this on the critic F. R. Leavis, who is obliquely derided in *The Shadow of the Sun* and named and shamed in *Still Life* and *Possession*.

Wordsworth and Coleridge in their Time (1970). Republished as *Unruly Times* in 1989. An account of the two poets' close personal acquaintance, as well as a study of their work, which has a significant connection with *Possession* (see Section 2 of this Guide).

Passions of the Mind: Selected Writings (1991). This work marks Byatt's escape from under the shadow of Leavis and the transition to a more "writerly" criticism which conveys her enthusiasm for admired writers, who include Robert Browing, George Eliot and Toni Morrison. She also writes on Van Gogh, Freud and post-structuralist literary theory. It is serious and erudite work, but idiosyncratic in its eclecticism, even bearing in mind that it comprises a collection of essays rather than a monograph.

Imagining Characters: Six Conversations about Women Writers, with Ignes Sôdré (1995). The women writers include, from the nineteenth century: Jane Austen, Charlotte Brontë and George Elliot, and from the twentieth, Iris Murdoch and Toni Morrison. The way that Byatt and Sôdré discuss fictional characters, as critic Lorna Sage put it, is to talk about them as real people. This demonstrates Byatt's recognition of the traditional pleasures of reading and suggests her continued commitment to the imaginative realization of character.

On Histories and Stories: Selected Essays (2000). This collection includes a study of modern British historical fiction, European storytelling and the *Arabian Nights*. It is of most relevance to *Possession*, which Byatt discusses along with other contemporary examples, and in some senses comprises a defense of the novel against critics who include committed social realist Margaret Drabble. One of the modern historical novels she discusses is John Fowles' *The French Lieutenant's Woman*, to which *Possession* is often compared because of the historical parallel between pairs of twentieth-century and Victorian lovers. It becomes clear here, however, that Fowles' novel was a negative model.

Romantic and Victorian Poetry

The following poems will convey something of the forms, themes and imagery characteristic of the nineteenth-century poets, and are chosen as particularly relevant to the poems in *Possession*:

Samuel Taylor Coleridge, "Christabel"
Robert Browning, especially "Childe Roland to the Dark Tower Came," *Caliban upon Setebos, Mr Sludge, the "Medium," Fra Lippo Lippi*
Alfred, Lord Tennyson, especially *Maud: A Monodrama; In Memoriam; The Lady of Shalott*
Emily Dickinson, *Poems*
Christina Rossetti, *Introspective; In the Round Tower at Jhansi; Winter: My Secret;* "The Heart Knoweth Its Own Bitterness"; *Goblin Market.*

Regarding Byatt's allusion to diverse texts across literary history, a comparable literary text is T. S. Elliot's *The Waste Land* (1922). This is a modernist poem, which is stuffed with literary allusion, lacks narrative coherence, and caused much confusion on initial publication. In a later version, Elliot added notes, attributing many of the quotations, which he called "a piece of bogus scholarship."

Twentieth-Century Criticism and Theory

For an idea of F. R. Leavis's self-assured and sometimes peremptory value judgments on literary texts see *Revaluation: Tradition and Development in English Poetry* (1936) or *The Common Pursuit* (1952). For examples of French feminist writing of the type which informs the discourse of Fergus, Maud, and particularly Leonora, see Hélène Cixous, "Sorties" in *The Newly Born Woman*, with Catherine Clément (Manchester University Press, 1986). Byatt's acknowledgements also mention the post Freudian Jacques Lacan, *Ecrits*, translated by Alan Sheridan (Tavistock Publications, 1977).

On postmodernity (the condition of knowledge in the late twentieth-century), the classic text is Jean-Francois Lyotard's *The Postmodern Condition: A Report on Knowledge*, translated by Geoff Bennington (Manchester University Press, 1984).

Contemporary Fiction

Margaret Drabble, *A Summer Bird Cage* (1963). This novel by Byatt's sister focuses on two sisters, both recently graduated from Oxford University, from the point of view of the younger. This novel demonstrates a similar preoccupation with the contemporary woman's role as Byatt's "Frederica" trilogy. In Drabble's novel, the elder sister, a great beauty, solves the problem by getting married, while the younger attempts to make it on her own. Drabble's next novel, *The Garrick Year* (1964) deals with the tribulations of a young mother forced to leave a successful career in the media and follow her actor-husband. *The Millstone* (1965) examines the predicament of an unmarried pregnant research student. Drabble's fiction, which is thematically and stylistically more consistent than Byatt's, can be classified as feminist social realism. Drabble's latest novel, *The Peppered Moth*, is closely based on the life of Byatt's mother, a fact which has caused Byatt some annoyance as reported in the British Press, which suggests a tit-for-tat battle going on, as the title story of *Sugar and Other Stories* fictionalizes their family history and father's death. Comparison with Drabble annoys Byatt, who complains that her fiction is sometimes not considered on its own merits, but the two unsurprisingly share preoccupation with the condition of educated women in post-war Britain, particularly in their earlier novels allowing some obvious connections to be drawn. For a short comparative account see Joanne V. Creighton, "Sisterly Symbiosis: Margaret Drabble's *The Waterfall* and A. S. Byatt's *The Game* in *Mosaic* 20 (Winter 1987), pp. 15–29 and Ewa Melnic's "Images of Women in Fiction: The novels of F. Weldon, M. Drabble and A. S. Byatt" in *English Studies* (Torun, Poland) 4 (1994), pp. 15–21.

Unlike Drabble, Iris Murdoch, has been a significant and ac-knowledged influence on Byatt's thinking and writing. As well as *Degrees of Freedom*, Byatt produced a short study of Murdoch's work for the British Council's Writers and their Work Series in 1976. Murdoch is another intellectual writer, whose moral philo-sophical training informs both her literary criticism and fiction, though unlike Byatt she makes a clear theoretical distinction be-tween literary and critical writing. The hero of Murdoch's first novel *Under the Net* (1954), is a translator who establishes his identity as a writer. As well as following the travails of the slightly feckless hero, the novel addresses questions of language after Cambridge philoso-pher Wittgenstein. Both the central theme and the linguistic pre-occupations of the novel are echoed in Byatt's *The Shadow of the Sun*. Much of Murdoch's work is informed by both the thought and imagery of classical and existentialist philosophy, particulary from the texts of Plato and Sartre, both "literary" philosophers. There is a scene in *A Fairly Honourable Defeat* (1970), in which one of the characters suffers a kind of existential fit preceded by a vision of blinding light. Her later novels, such as *The Black Prince* and *The Philosopher's Pupil* combine a broadly realistic mode with elements of metafiction.

Postmodern Fiction

Neither Drabble nor Murdoch classify as postmodernists, although there are postmodern elements in Murdoch's novels. John Fowles, *The French Lieutenant's Woman* (1969) has often been compared to *Possession* by commentators and there are some obvious parallels between the two novels. The first of these is that the novel contains two romance narratives: of clandestine Victorian love and of contemporary adultery. The main Victorian narrative is written in the realist style of a Victorian novel, until the narrator begins to intrude and question narrative conventions. There is a chapter on Victorian sex, masquerading as a sophisticated post-Freudian essay, but suggesting a critique of contemporary sexual morality. In addition "real" figures from literary history (the Rossettis) pop up in the text.

Another novel which is a precursor to *Possession* in its treatment of narrative time is Graham Swift's, *Waterland* (1983), shortlisted for the Booker Prize. This novel, whose narrative present is the 1950s, explores the relationship between the individual history of its protagonists and much earlier historical events. The narrative chronology is manipulated in order to foreground parallels between the events in different historical periods.

A novelist whose professional interest in literary theory informs his fiction is David Lodge. *Small World* (1984) shares other features with *Possession*; it is an allusive intertextual campus comedy, which alludes to archetypal quest and romance narratives, as well as contemporary literary theory. Lodge has written two other metafictional campus comedies which draw on contemporary literary theory: *Changing Places* (1975) and *Nice Work* (1988). The latter also alludes to and mimics the structure of the nineteenth-century novel.

Michèle Roberts, who has written admiringly on Byatt in *Food, Sex & God*, uses literary history as an inspiration for her fiction. *Fair Exchange* (Little, Brown, 1999) was inspired by the lives of two eighteenth-century figures: the Romantic poet William Wordsworth, and the early feminist Mary Wollstonecraft, but focuses on Wordsworth's historically marginalized mistress, Annette Vallon and a fictional character loosely based on Wollstonecraft. Roberts constructs a story round specific historical detail as well as creating a fictional world. She has other shared interests with Byatt; in her novel *Daughters of the House* (1992) the historical past "haunts" the present and directs the action of the protagonists. "Classic" studies of postmodernist fiction include Linda Hutcheon's *Narcissistic Narrative: The Metafictional Paradox* (London: Methuen, 1984) and *A Poetics of Postmodernism* (1988); Brian McHale, *Postmodernist Fiction* (London: Routledge, 1987).

Byatt has identified herself as a "European" writer, in part because of her interest in the archetypal forms of European folk and fairy tale. Byatt's interest in fairy tale was shared by Angela Carter, who in *The Bloody Chamber and Other Stories* (1979), undertakes a feminist, postmodernist rewriting of traditional fairy tales, but in both cases the models are pan-European rather than British, and a prime literary influence, Grimm, is German. Byatt has been influenced by Italian essayist and novelist Italo Calvino, who has written on Italian folk tales, and also published a work of "extreme" postmodern metafiction in *If On a Winter's Night a Traveller*, translated by William Weaver (1981). She also admires the Argentinian postmodern writer, Jorge Luis Borges. *Possession* has been compared with his work, as has her later novel *The Biographer's Tale*. Borges' short stories, occasionally masquerading as essays, are often set in a mythic past and are allegories on metaphysical themes: questions of knowledge and the relationship between fact and fiction. See *Collected Fictions*, translated by Andrew Hurley (London: Penguin, 1998). Umberto Eco is an Italian academic and novelist. *The Name of the Rose*, translated by William Weaver (1983) can be compared to *Possession* in several respects; it is a postmodern literary detective story and medieaval mystery, whose holy grail is a book, as well an allegory which addresses postmodern questions of knowledge.

Bibliography

Reviews and Interviews

Michael Dirda, "The incandescent spell of *Possession*." *Washington Post* (17 October 1990).

Harriett Gilbert. "Primitive fear of possession." *Independent on Sunday* (2 July 2000).

Richard Jenkyns. "Disinterring Buried Lives." *Times Literary Supplement* (2 March 1990).

Peter Kemp. "An Extravaganza of Victoriana." *Sunday Times* (4 March 1990).

Christopher Lehmann-Haupt. "Books of the Times: When there was such a thing as romantic love." *New York Times* (25 October 1990).

Nicola Murphy. "A romance of literary criticism." *Times* (1 March 1990).

Jay Parini. "Unearthing the Secret Lover." *New York Times* (21 October 1990).

Mervyn Rothstein. "Best Seller Breaks Rule on Crossing Atlantic." *New York Times* (31 January 1991).

Mira Stout. "What Possessed A. S. Byatt?" *New York Times* (26 May 1991).

Nicolas Tredell. *Conversations with Critics*. Manchester: Carcanet, 1994: 58–74.

Terry Trucco. "Brit Wit's Lit Hit: Antonia's anonymous no more." *Wall Street Journal* (6 December 1990).

Websites

www.asbyatt.com. The official website containing details of forthcoming events and publications and including a substantial annotated primary and secondary bibliography.

www.randomhouse.com/vintage/read/possession

Byatt's American publisher's *Possesion* site containing questions, discussion topics, author biography, and suggested reading, designed to "enhance" reading group discussions.

Criticism

Jackie Buxton. "What's Love Got to Do with It?" Postmodernism and *Possession*. *English Studies in Canada* 22 (June 1996): 199–219.

Giuliana Giobbi. "Know the Past, Know Thyself: Literary Pursuits and Quests for Identity in A. S. Byatt's *Possession* and in Francesca Duranti's *Effetti Personali*." *Journal of European Studies* 24 (March 1994): 41–54.

Julian Gitzen. "A. S. Byatt's Self-Mirroring Art", *Critique* 36:2 (1995): 83–95.

Frederick M. Holmes. "The Historical Imagination and the Victorian Past: A. S. Byatt's *Possession*. *English Studies in Canada* 20 (September 1994): 319–34.

Ann Hulbert. "The Great Ventriloquist: A. S. Byatt's *Possession: A Romance*" in *Contemporary British Women Writers*, ed. Robert E. Hosmer Jr. New York: St Martin's Press, 1993: 55–65.

Del Ivan Janik. "No End of History: Evidence from the Contemporary English Novel." *Twentieth Century Literature* 41 (Summer 1995): 160–89.

Olga Kenyon. "A. S. Byatt" in *Women Novelists Today: A Survey of Writing in the Seventies and Eighties*. New York: St Martin's Press, 1998: 51–84.

Michael Levenson. "The Religion of Fiction." *New Republic* 209 (2 August 1993): 41–44.

Helen E. Mundler. " 'Intratextual Passages': *The Glass Coffin* in the Work of A. S. Byatt." *Etudes Britanniques Contemporaines* 11 (1997): 1–8.

Michèle Roberts. "The Passionate Reader: *Possession* and Romance" in *Food, Sex & God: On Inspiration and Writing* (London: Virago, 1998), pp. 47–69.

Susanne Schmid. "Metafictional Explorations of Realism: The Novels of A. S. Byatt." *Hard Times* 56 (Spring 1996): 8–11.

Dana Shiller. "The Redemptive Past in the Neo-Victorian Novel." *Studies in the Novel* 29:4 (Winter 1997): 538–60.

Susan Stock Thomas. "Writing the Self and Other in Byatt's *Possession* and in the Browning/Barrett Correspondence." *Studies in Browning and His Circle* 20 (1993): 88–94.

Richard Todd. *A. S. Byatt*. Plymouth: Northcote House, 1997.

———. "A. S. Byatt's *Possession*: An International Literary Success" in *Consuming Fictions: The Booker Prize and Fiction in Britain Today* (London: Bloomsbury, 1996), pp. 25–54.

Celia M. Wallhead. *The Old, the New and the Metaphor: A Critical Study of the Novels of A. S. Byatt*. Atlanta, London, Sydney: Atlanta, 1999.

Notes

1. Many of the figures quoted in this Section are taken from Richard Todd's "A. S. Byatt's *Possession*: An International Literary Success" in *Consuming Fictions: The Booker Prize and Fiction in Britain Today* (London: Bloomsbury, 1996), pp. 25–54.